THE ULTIMATE GUITAR CHORD PICTURE CASEBOOK

by **Don Latarski**

Photos and Graphics by Kathy Kifer and Jane Schneider
Project Manager: Aaron Stang
Cover Art Design: Carmen Fortunato and Candy Woolley
Cover Guitar Photo: Taylor 812CE Courtesy of Taylor Guitars

Navigating through the seemingly endless number of chords on the guitar can feel overwhelming to the beginning student. There are many ways to combine the notes that make up a chord and still more ways to finger them. So where to start?

Most people begin by learning a handful of chords in 1st position. This is the area of the guitar where the strings are at their maximum length. A vibrating string sounds best when it's long as opposed to short. Most chords have more presence and sustain when played in the lower positions. And the best sounding chords are ones that incorporate open strings.

There are three general groups of chords. Each group produces a certain sound or feeling. The major chords make us feel good, satisfied, at peace, or restful. Minor chords produce reflective, pensive, or sad feelings. The last group, called dominant chords, is the largest group and contains the chords that produce agitation, discord, and tension. These are generalizations but do serve as a good starting place in organizing the different chord families.

Most songs contain one or more chords from each of these groups. So it makes sense to begin learning chords from each group. You'll need to know a couple of different ways to play a major triad, minor triad, and dominant 7th chord. At a minimum, you'll want to learn chord forms with the root notes on strings 6 and 5.

Hand shapes:

There are a really only a small number of different ways of holding your hand when you form chords. The thumb should be in the "hitch-hiking" position, fully outstretched. With most chords, your thumb will be in the middle to upper part on the back of the neck.

Fully extended thumb

Incorrect thumb position

Correct thumb position

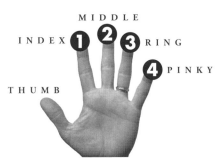

As a general rule, your thumb is positioned in such a way as to balance the pressure from the fingers placed farthest down and up the neck. Notice in this barre chord how the thumb is centered between the first and third fingers. A triangle is formed between the first, third, and thumb. The relationship

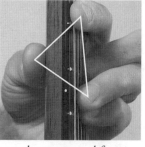

between the fingers and thumb balances the energy and force needed to play a chord with the least amount of effort.

There are a number of different standard chord "grips." By becoming familiar with them, you'll be able to play any chord in this book quickly. One of the most basic hand shapes involves playing one note with each finger with minimal finger stretches.

Many chords in this book use this hand shape.

Another variation to the one-finger-per-string approach is used to play chords that span four or more frets. For most people, these chords are difficult to play. Some of these chords are included in this book because they sound good and in some cases are the logical choice for a particular chord type. To play these stretchy chords, you'll need your thumb in the middle of the neck. If your thumb is wrapped around to the 6th string, you won't be able to spread your hand out and make the stretch. Improper thumb position is often the reason people can't spread out their fingers.

Stretchy hand position

The anatomy of the hand makes most fingerings quite straightforward. However, a few chords require a "cross-finger" technique. A good example of this type of chord occurs in the minor 6th chord, 5th-string root. In this chord, the fourth finger crosses in front of the first and third fingers.

Cross-finger position

Another common chord fingering involves some type of barre. A barre chord involves holding down two or more strings with the same finger. Any finger can do the barring, but the index finger usually is assigned this task.

Many beginning guitarists have difficulty with the barre chord, and for good reason. The most common major barre chord is also one of the most difficult since you have to hold down notes on strings 1, 2, and 6 with the index finger.

Full barre chord

My suggestion for beginners with this type of chord is to begin trying to get the lower notes to come out clearly first. Just focus on the 6th, 5th, 4th, and 3rd strings. Notice that you're not actually playing a barre chord. As you gain experience and strength, you can begin refining the barre to include some of the other notes.

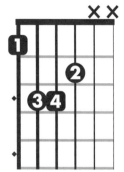

The beginner's "barre" chord

A technique that is different from the standard way of positioning your fretting hand involves laying certain fingers on their sides. This technique will allow you to spread fingers 2 and 3—useful for playing certain chords. To achieve this position, tilt your fingers back toward the tuners. This tilt-back technique may feel a bit awkward at first, but it's one of the guitar playing tricks that the pros all know.

The "tilt-back" technique

Interpreting the chord diagrams:

There are two ways to view each chord: graphically with a photo and a corresponding chord grid. Each of these graphics presents a different view as to how each chord could be played. There is a literal view—how I hold my hand when I play the chord—and a more detailed view presented on the chord grid. The photo can really help since you get an idea of how your hand might look when you play the chord. Everyone's hand anatomy is a little different, so your hand may not look exactly like mine.

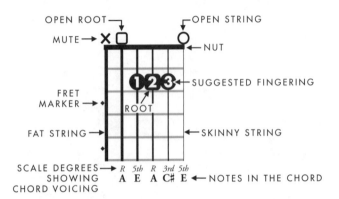

The chord diagram shows a suggested fingering, which notes are to be played, which strings to avoid or to mute (shown with an "X" above the string), inclusion of any open strings, the location of the chord root, the scale degrees that make up the chord, and the pitch names. This is more information than you need to play the chord, but it's there in case you're interested in learning more about the theory of the chord. (See the later section on chord theory.)

Simplifying the chords:

There are chords in here that you may find very difficult to play. Take heart. You can simplify nearly any chord by simply leaving some of the notes out. There just wasn't room in this book to show every possible way to finger a given chord, so it's up to you to experiment with these chords. It's pretty safe to say that most chords can be reduced down to two or three notes without sacrificing the chord's personality. Once you understand that the personality of a chord is contained in the 3rd and 7th scale degrees, you can begin omitting notes.

As a general rule, you can first eliminate the 5th of any chord unless it is a ♭5 or ♯5. You can also leave out the root. Keep the last chord extension. For example, if the chord is some type of 9th, you need to include this 9th in the chord along with the 3rd and 7th. If the chord is a 13th, make sure you keep the 3rd, 7th, and 13th. In this way, you can greatly simplify nearly any chord.

See the photos on this page to learn how this difficult chord can be simplified.

Full barre chord

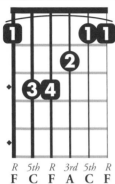

R	5th	R	3rd	5th	R
F	C	F	A	C	F

Alternative 1

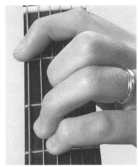

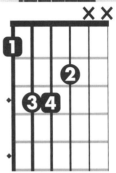

Alternative 2

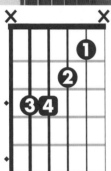

Alternative 3

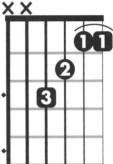

Alternative 4

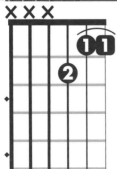

Alternative 5

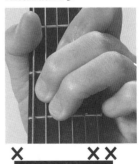

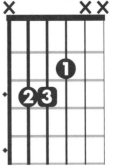

Muting strings:

Many chords are made up of notes that are not on adjacent strings. In such cases an "X" will be placed over that string, indicating that you aren't supposed to hit that string. However, this can be difficult if you are strumming with a pick. It's not so difficult for finger-style players.

Muting is the technique that allows you to strum all six strings without making the chord sound bad. The fingers of the fretting hand muffle or dampen the strings that are not used in the chord. The beauty of this technique is that you get can add percussive energy to the chord.

It's difficult to see the muting taking place from the chord pictures. The trick to muting is finding just the right way of positioning the fretting hand so that the side of one or more fingers lightly touches the string to be muted. This technique takes practice, but it's worth the effort since the payoff is substantial. Muting notes is essential to developing a high-energy rhythm guitar technique.

Alternate fingerings:

The fingerings suggested in this book are the standard ones. However, don't be afraid to try different ones. I often use my thumb to play bass notes on string 6. This works for me but is difficult for most people. Experiment with different hand positions. If you're experiencing any sort of pain in your fretting hand, stop playing and get some advice from a trained teacher. You may be doing something wrong that could result in damage to your hand.

Finding the right chord in this book:

You must first be able to identify what type of chord you want. In order to do this, you have to know if the chord is major, minor, or dominant. The section on understanding chord symbols will help you.

In most cases, you'll want to play the first or second form shown. The reason for this is that the first and second chords are going to be found in the lower positions on the guitar. This means the strings will be longer and chords will be fuller and richer. If you don't like the sound of the chord, try one of the others. Try leaving out one or more of the notes. Look to see that you're not holding down notes that you don't need. Also, make sure you're muting the strings that require silencing.

Understanding chord symbols:

When a chord appears in a song, it is represented with a chord symbol. Unfortunately, it is not uncommon for the same chord to be represented with a variety of symbols. This non-standardization of chord symbols makes it difficult at times to identify what chord is needed.

This list will help you identify the correct type of chord so that you can look it up with confidence. All examples are based on a C root note.

chord name	symbol(s)
C major triad	C, Cmaj
C major 6	C6, Cma6, Cmaj6
C major 7th	Cma7, CM7, Cmaj7, C△7
C major add 9th	C(9), Cadd9, Cma(add9)
C major 9th	Cmaj9, CM9, Cma9, C△9
C major7 sharp 11th	Cmaj7♯11, CM7♯11, Cma7♯11, C△7♯11
C major7 flat 5th	Cmaj7♭5, CM7♭5, Cma7♭5, C△7♭5
C major 6/9	C6/9, Cmaj6/9, CM69
C suspended 2	Csus2
C suspended 4	Csus4
C minor triad	Cm, Cmi, Cmin, C-
C minor 6th	Cm6, Cmi6, Cmin6, C-6
C minor 7th	Cm7, Cmi7, Cmin7, C-7
C minor 7th flat 5th	Cm7♭5, Cmi7♭5, Cmin7♭5, C-7♭5, Cø7
C minor 9th	Cm9, Cmi9, Cmin9, C-9
C minor-major 7th	Cm(maj7), Cmi(ma7), Cm♯7, C-(♯7), Cm♮7
C minor add 9th	Cm(9), Cm(add9), Cmi(add9), Cmin(add9), C-add9
C minor 11th	Cm11, Cmi11th, Cmin11, C-11
C minor 13th	Cm13, Cmi13th, Cmin13, C-13
C dominant 7th	C7, Cdom7
C dominant 9th	C9, Cdom9
C dominant 7, suspended 4th	C7sus4, Cdom7sus4
C dominant 9, suspended 4th	C9sus4, Cdom9sus4
C dominant 13th	C13, Cdom13
C dominant 7th, flat 5th	C7(♭5), C7♭5, C7-5, Cdom7-5
C dominant 7th, sharp 5th	C7(♯5), C7♯5, C7+5, Cdom7+5
C dominant 7th, flat 9th	C7(♭9), C7♭9, C7-9, Cdom7-9
C dominant 7th, sharp 9th	C7(♯9), C7♯9, C7+9, Cdom7+9
C dominant 9th, flat 5th	C9(♭5), C9♭5, C9-5, Cdom9-5
C dominant 9th, sharp 5th	C9(♯5), C9♯5, C9+5, Cdom9+5
C diminished 7th	Cdim7, C°7

Basic chord theory:

You don't have to know squat about music theory to use this book, but it won't hurt. At the top of each page next to the name of the chord is a series of numbers. The major 7th chord lists 1-3-5-7. These numbers refer to the correct scale degrees needed to build that particular type of chord. The actual scale degree names are there as well. These correspond to the scale degrees from the key that you are in.

For example, a Cmaj7 chord is made up of C-E-G-B. This means that the chord is built by using the 1st, 3rd, 5th, and 7th notes from the C major scale. These scale degrees can be arranged in any order on the guitar. The resulting chord would still be a Cmaj7.

When we talk about the order of notes in a chord, it is called *voicing*. The voicing of a chord is always described from the lowest sounding note up to the highest. Voicing is very important to how pleasant a chord sounds. A bad voicing can result in a chord that is unclear, muddy, or even harsh. This book contains only common voicings. Many other voicings do exist for all of these chords.

When the root of the chord (listed as an uppercase "R" under one or more strings) is the lowest sounding note, the chord is said to be in *root position*. Most of the chords in this book are in root position. Root position is the most common way to play a chord and is also the most stable and grounded. A few chords aren't in root position. These chords are in *inversion*. Inverted chord forms are less stable sounding than root position chords but are sometimes more convenient to play. This is why they are included in this book.

Understanding chord formulas and voicings gives a person a great deal of control over what's being played. You can manipulate the chord shapes as you're playing as opposed to being a slave to memorized hand shapes.

Chords can be known by more than one name depending on what key the song is in. When a note has more than one name, it is called *enharmonic equivalent*. For example, a C♯ will sound the same as D♭. Here is a list of the most common enharmonic equivalent notes:

A♯ = B♭

B♯ = C

C♯ = D♭

D♯ = E♭

F♯ = G♭

G♯ = A♭

Notation conventions:

Most people are familiar with the standard symbols used to modify pitches. The flat symbol (♭) lowers a note one half step—the equivalent of one fret on the guitar. This makes a pitch lower in sound. To lower a pitch a whole step (same as two half steps), a double flat symbol is used (♭♭).

To raise a pitch by one half step, the sharp symbol is used (♯). To raise a pitch a whole step, a double sharp symbol is used (×). In order to avoid confusion, in this book a double sharp note is indicated with two sharp symbols (♯♯).

Want more chords?

When you're ready to move on to the next stage in your chord quest, consider these publications:

An Introduction to Chord Theory, by Don Latarski,
  Warner Bros. Publications, $9.95.

Chord Orbits, by Don Latarski,
  Warner Bros. Publications, $12.95.

Moveable Chords, by Don Latarski,
  Warner Bros. Publications, $9.95.

Chord Embellishments, by Don Latarski,
  Warner Bros. Publications, $9.95

First Chords, by Don Latarski,
  Warner Bros. Publications, $9.95.

Jazz Chords, by Don Latarski,
  Warner Bros. Publications, $9.95.

Barre Chords, by Don Latarski,
  Warner Bros. Publications, $9.95.

Blues Chords, by Don Latarski,
  Warner Bros. Publications, $9.95.

The Ultimate Guitar Chord Big Book, by Don Latarski,
  Warner Bros. Publications, $24.95.

Take a look at all of these books or ask questions of the author by going to:

www.DonLatarski.com

Table of Contents

A

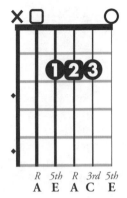

R *5th* *R* *3rd* *5th*
A E A C E

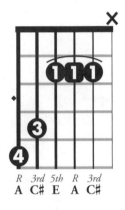

R *3rd* *5th* *R* *3rd*
A C# E A C#

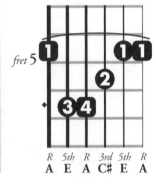

fret 5

R *5th* *R* *3rd* *5th* *R*
A E A C# E A

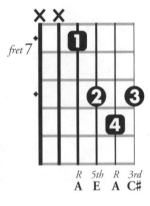

fret 7

R *5th* *R* *3rd*
A E A C#

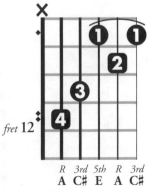

fret 12

R *3rd* *5th* *R* *3rd*
A C# E A C#

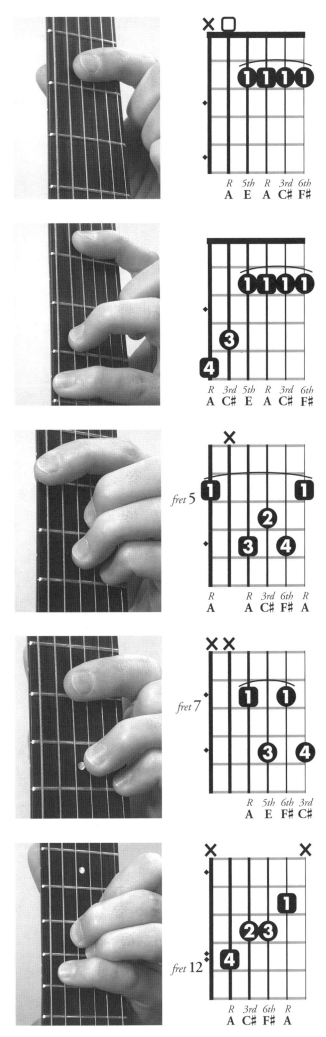

R *5th* *R* *3rd* *6th*
A E A C# F#

R *3rd* *5th* *R* *3rd* *6th*
A C# E A C# F#

fret 5

R   *R* *3rd* *6th* *R*
A   A C# F# A

fret 7

R *5th* *6th* *3rd*
A E F# C#

fret 12

R *3rd* *6th* *R*
A C# F# A

Amaj7

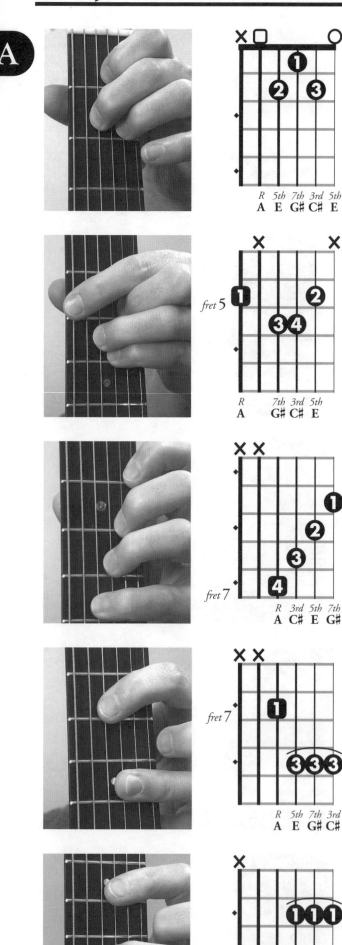

R 5th 7th 3rd 5th
A E G# C# E

fret 5

R   7th 3rd 5th
A   G#   C#   E

fret 7

R 3rd 5th 7th
A C# E G#

fret 7

R 5th 7th 3rd
A E G# C#

fret 12

R 3rd 5th 7th 3rd
A C# E G# C#

SCALE DEGREES: *R 3rd 5th 9th*
CHORD TONES: A C# E B

A(9)

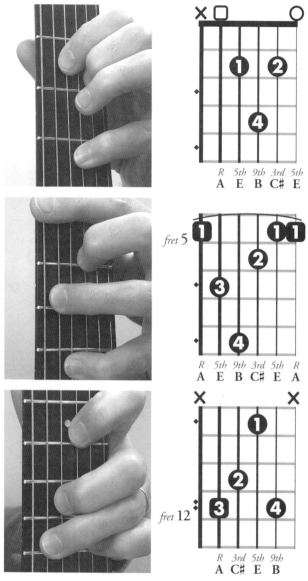

R	5th	9th	3rd	5th
A	E	B	C#	E

fret 5

R	5th	9th	3rd	5th	R
A	E	B	C#	E	A

fret 12

R	3rd	5th	9th
A	C#	E	B

SCALE DEGREES: *R 3rd 5th 7th 9th*
CHORD TONES: A C# E G# B

Amaj9

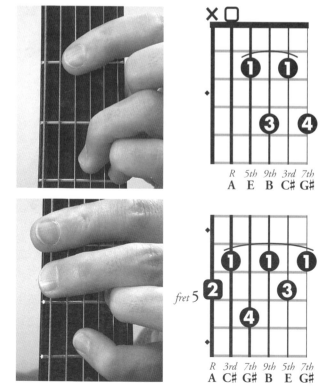

R	5th	9th	3rd	7th
A	E	B	C#	G#

fret 5

R	3rd	7th	9th	5th	7th
A	C#	G#	B	E	G#

Amaj7(#11)

SCALE DEGREES: *R 3rd 5th 7th #11th*
CHORD TONES: A C# E G# D#

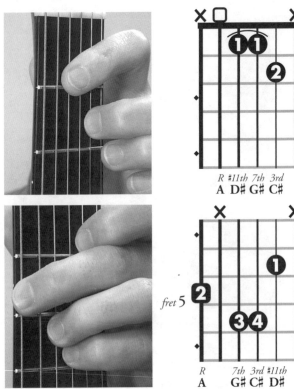

R #11th 7th 3rd
A D# G# C#

fret 5

R   7th 3rd #11th
A   G# C# D#

A6/9

SCALE DEGREES: *R 3rd 5th 6th 9th*
CHORD TONES: A C# E F# B

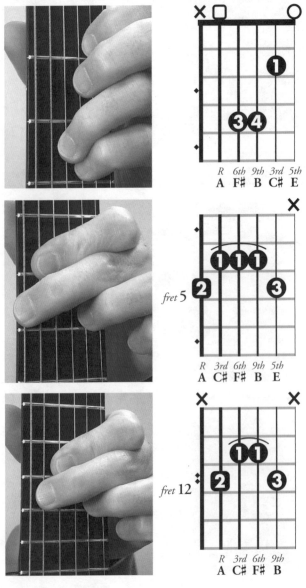

R 6th 9th 3rd 5th
A F# B C# E

fret 5

R   3rd 6th 9th 5th
A   C# F# B E

fret 12

R 3rd 6th 9th
A C# F# B

SCALE DEGREES: *R 2nd 5th*
CHORD TONES: A B E

Asus2

R	5th	R	2nd	5th
A	E	A	B	E

fret 5

R	5th	2nd
A	E	B

SCALE DEGREES: *R 4th 5th*
CHORD TONES: A D E

Asus4

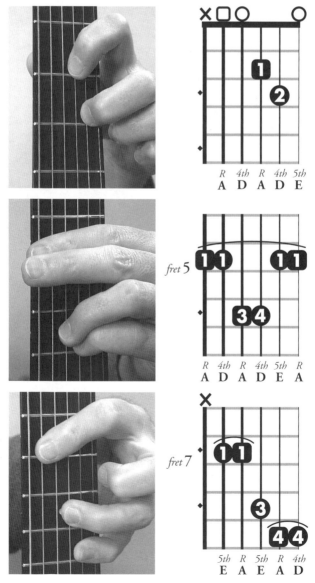

R	4th	R	4th	5th
A	D	A	D	E

fret 5

R	4th	R	4th	5th	R
A	D	A	D	E	A

fret 7

5th	R	5th	R	4th
E	A	E	A	D

Am

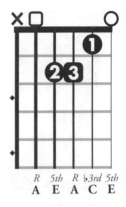

SCALE DEGREES: *R ♭3rd 5th*
CHORD TONES: A C E

×

```
    ○
  ①
②③
```

R	5th	R	♭3rd	5th
A	E	A	C	E

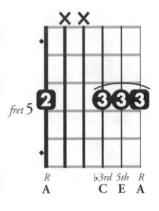

× ×

fret 5
```
②    ③③③
```

R		♭3rd	5th	R
A		C	E	A

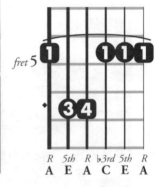

fret 5
```
①    ①①①
  ③④
```

R	5th	R	♭3rd	5th	R
A	E	A	C	E	A

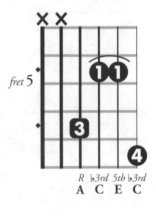

× ×

fret 5
```
   ①①
 ③
      ④
```

R	♭3rd	5th	♭3rd
A	C	E	C

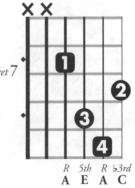

× ×

fret 7
```
 ①
    ②
  ③
  ④
```

R	5th	R	♭3rd
A	E	A	C

20   *The Ultimate Guitar Chord Casebook*

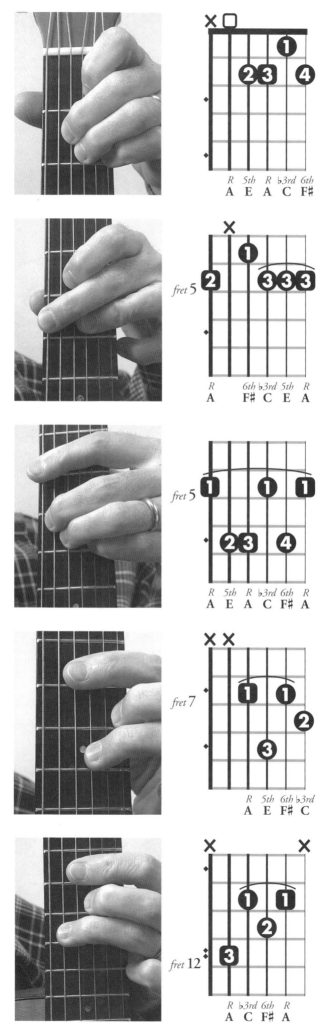

R	5th	R ♭3rd	6th
A	E	A C	F♯

fret 5

| R | | 6th ♭3rd 5th | R |
| A | | F♯ C E | A |

fret 5

| R | 5th | R ♭3rd | 6th | R |
| A | E | A C | F♯ | A |

fret 7

| R | 5th | 6th ♭3rd |
| A | E | F♯ C |

fret 12

| R | ♭3rd | 6th | R |
| A | C | F♯ | A |

Am7

SCALE DEGREES: R ♭3rd 5th ♭7th
CHORD TONES: A C E G

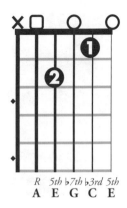

R 5th ♭7th ♭3rd 5th
A E G C E

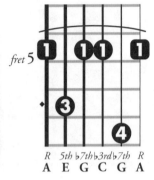

fret 5

R 5th ♭7th ♭3rd ♭7th R
A E G C G A

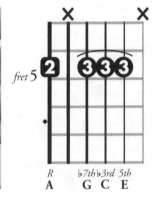

fret 5

R ♭7th ♭3rd 5th
A G C E

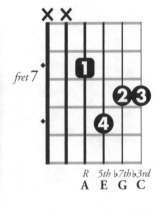

fret 7

R 5th ♭7th ♭3rd
A E G C

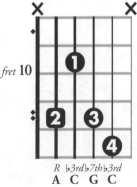

fret 10

R ♭3rd ♭7th ♭3rd
A C G C

SCALE DEGREES: *R ♭3rd ♭5th ♭7th*
CHORD TONES: A C E♭ G

Am7(♭5)

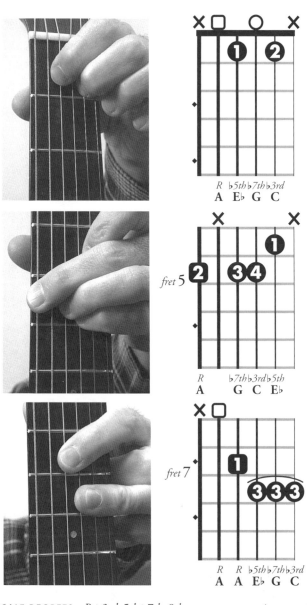

× □ ○ ×
1 2

R ♭5th ♭7th ♭3rd
A E♭ G C

× ×
2 3 4 1

fret 5

R ♭7th ♭3rd ♭5th
A G C E♭

× □
1
3 3 3

fret 7

R R ♭5th ♭7th ♭3rd
A A E♭ G C

SCALE DEGREES: *R ♭3rd 5th ♭7th 9th*
CHORD TONES: A C E G B

Am9

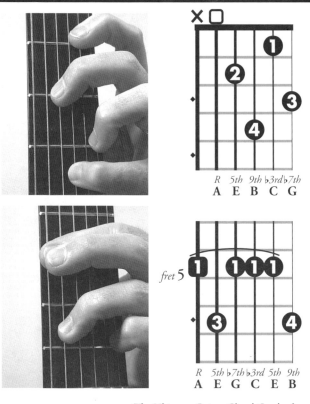

× □
1
2
3
4

R 5th 9th ♭3rd ♭7th
A E B C G

× □
1 1 1 1

fret 5

3 4

R 5th ♭7th ♭3rd 5th 9th
A E G C E B

Am(maj7)

SCALE DEGREES: R ♭3rd 5th 7th
CHORD TONES: A C E G#

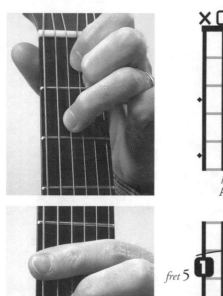

R 5th 7th ♭3rd 5th
A E G# C E

fret 5

R 5th 7th ♭3rd 5th R
A E G# C E A

Am(9)

SCALE DEGREES: R ♭3rd 5th 9th
CHORD TONES: A C E B

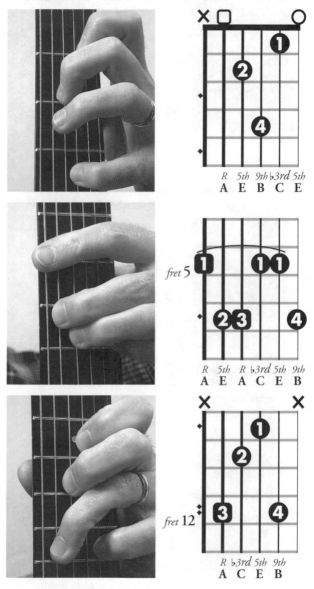

R 5th 9th ♭3rd 5th
A E B C E

fret 5

R 5th R ♭3rd 5th 9th
A E A C E B

fret 12

R ♭3rd 5th 9th
A C E B

SCALE DEGREES: *R ♭3rd 5th ♭7th 9th 11th*
CHORD TONES: A C E G B D

Am11

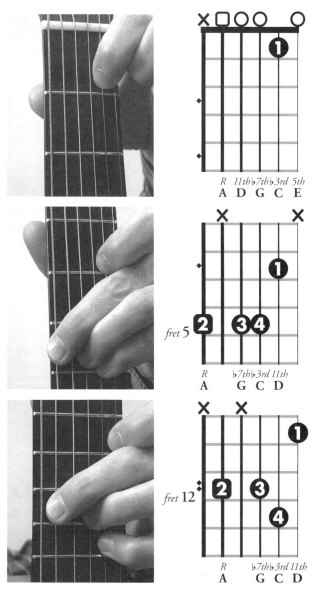

R   11th ♭7th 3rd 5th
A   D   G   C   E

fret 5

R   ♭7th ♭3rd 11th
A   G   C   D

fret 12

R   ♭7th ♭3rd 11th
A   G   C   D

SCALE DEGREES: *R ♭3rd 5th ♭7th 9th 11th 13th*
CHORD TONES: A C E G B D F♯

Am13

R   11th ♭7th 3rd 13th
A   D   G   C   F♯

fret 5

R   11th ♭7th ♭3rd 13th 9th
A   D   G   C   F♯ B

A7

SCALE DEGREES: *R 3rd 5th♭7th*
CHORD TONES: A C♯ E G

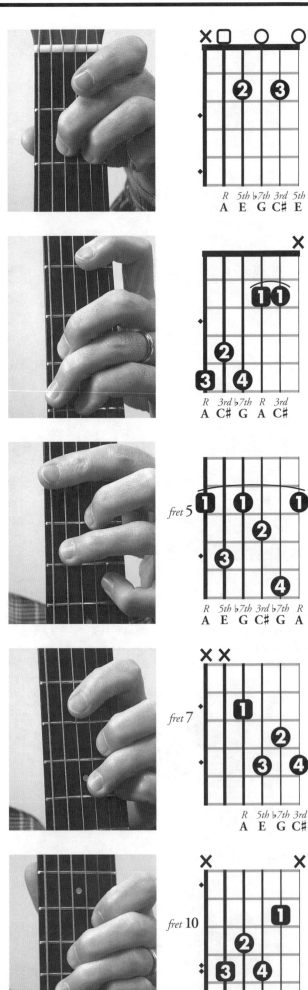

× □ ○ ○
② ③
R 5th ♭7th 3rd 5th
A E G C♯ E

×
① ①
② ④
③
R 3rd ♭7th R 3rd
A C♯ G A C♯

fret 5
① ① ①
②
③
④
R 5th ♭7th 3rd ♭7th R
A E G C♯ G A

× ×
fret 7
①
②
③ ④
R 5th ♭7th 3rd
A E G C♯

× ×
fret 10
①
②
③ ④
R 3rd ♭7th R
A C♯ G A

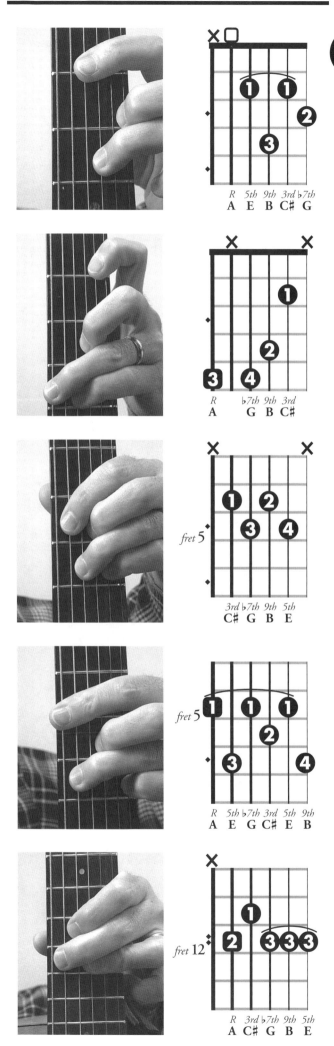

A7sus4

SCALE DEGREES: R 4th 5th ♭7th
CHORD TONES: A D E G

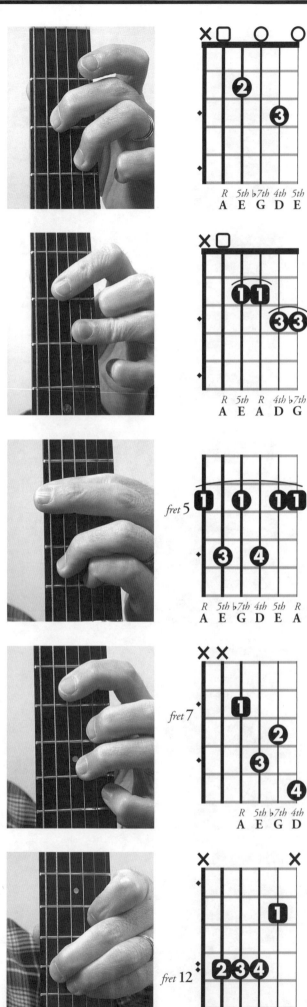

R 5th ♭7th 4th 5th
A E G D E

R 5th R 4th ♭7th
A E A D G

fret 5

R 5th ♭7th 4th 5th R
A E G D E A

fret 7

R 5th ♭7th 4th
A E G D

fret 12

R 4th ♭7th R
A D G A

SCALE DEGREES: *R 4th 5th ♭7th 9th*
CHORD TONES: A D E G B

A9sus4

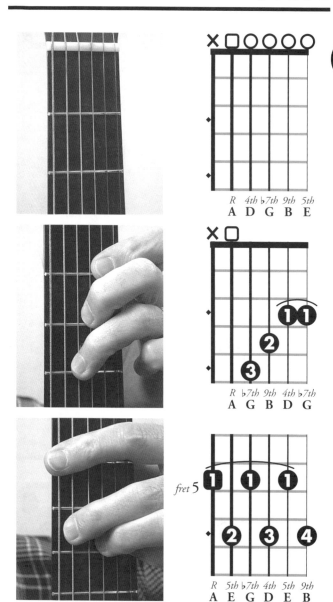

× □ ○ ○ ○ ○

R 4th ♭7th 9th 5th
A D G B E

× □

R ♭7th 9th 4th ♭7th
A G B D G

fret 5

R 5th ♭7th 4th 5th 9th
A E G D E B

SCALE DEGREES: *R 3rd 5th ♭7th 9th 11th 13th*
CHORD TONES: A C♯ E G B D F♯

A13

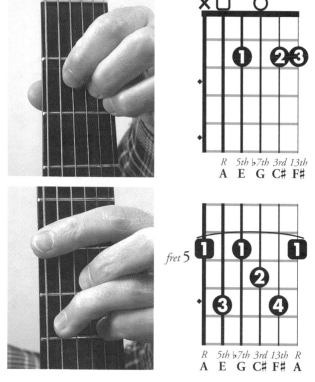

× □   ○

R 5th ♭7th 3rd 13th
A E G C♯ F♯

fret 5

R 5th ♭7th 3rd 13th R
A E G C♯ F♯ A

A7(♭5)

A

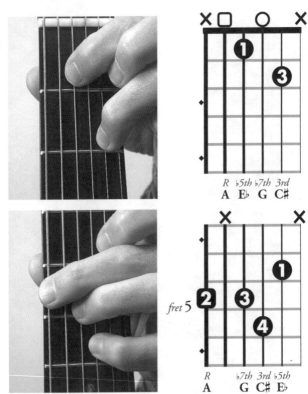

R ♭5th ♭7th 3rd
A E♭ G C#

fret 5

R ♭7th 3rd ♭5th
A G C# E♭

A7(♯5)

SCALE DEGREES: R 3rd #5th ♭7th
CHORD TONES: A C# E# G

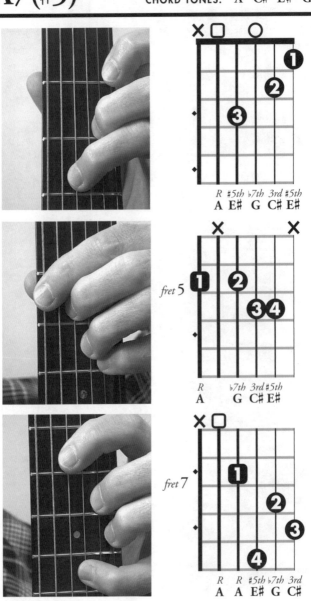

R #5th ♭7th 3rd #5th
A E# G C# E#

fret 5

R ♭7th 3rd #5th
A G C# E#

fret 7

R R #5th ♭7th 3rd
A A E# G C#

SCALE DEGREES: *R 3rd 5th ♭7th ♭9th*
CHORD TONES: A C# E G B♭

A7(♭9)

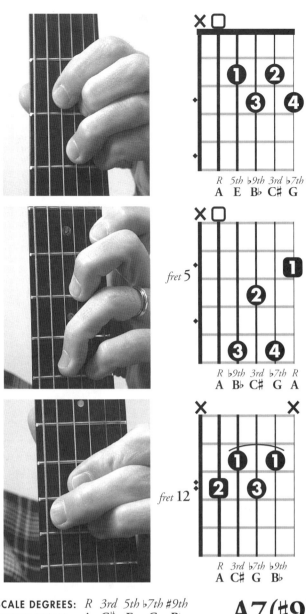

R 5th ♭9th 3rd ♭7th
A E B♭ C# G

fret 5

R ♭9th 3rd ♭7th R
A B♭ C# G A

fret 12

R 3rd ♭7th ♭9th
A C# G B♭

SCALE DEGREES: *R 3rd 5th ♭7th #9th*
CHORD TONES: A C# E G B♭

A7(#9)

fret 5

R 3rd ♭7th #9th 5th
A C# G B# E

fret 12

R 3rd ♭7th #9th
A C# G B#

The Ultimate Guitar Chord Casebook 31

A9(♭5)

SCALE DEGREES: *R 3rd ♭5th ♭7th 9th*
CHORD TONES: A C# E♭ G B

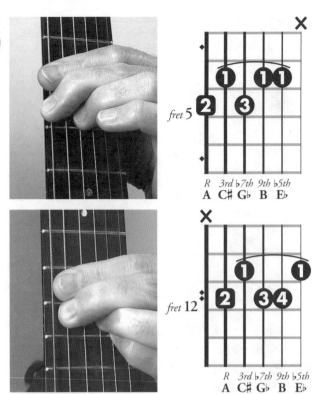

fret 5

R	3rd	♭7th	9th	♭5th
A	C#	G♭	B	E♭

fret 12

R	3rd	♭7th	9th	♭5th
A	C#	G♭	B	E♭

A9(#5)

SCALE DEGREES: *R 3rd #5th ♭7th 9th*
CHORD TONES: A C# E# G B

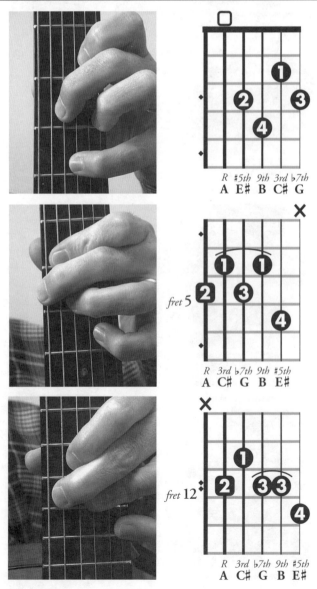

R	#5th	9th	3rd	♭7th
A	E#	B	C#	G

fret 5

R	3rd	♭7th	9th	#5th
A	C#	G	B	E#

fret 12

R	3rd	♭7th	9th	#5th
A	C#	G	B	E#

SCALE DEGREES: *R ♭3rd ♭5th ♭♭7th*
CHORD TONES: A C E♭ G♭

Adim7

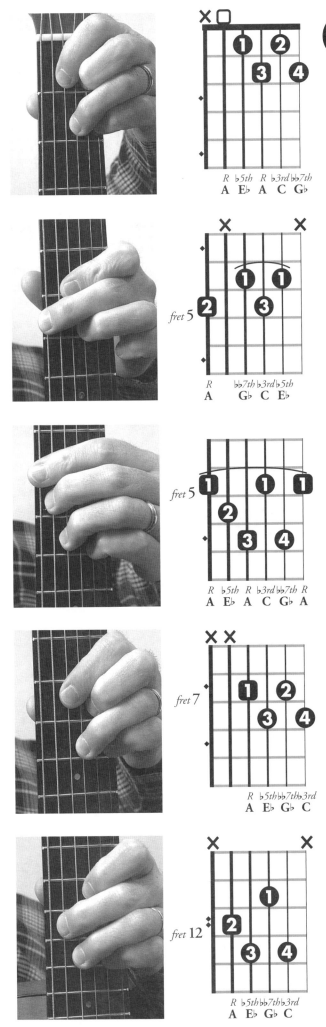

R ♭5th R ♭3rd ♭♭7th
A E♭ A C G♭

R ♭♭7th ♭3rd ♭5th
A G♭ C E♭

fret 5

R ♭5th R ♭3rd ♭♭7th R
A E♭ A C G♭ A

fret 5

R ♭5th ♭♭7th ♭3rd
A E♭ G♭ C

fret 7

R ♭5th ♭♭7th ♭3rd
A E♭ G♭ C

fret 12

B♭

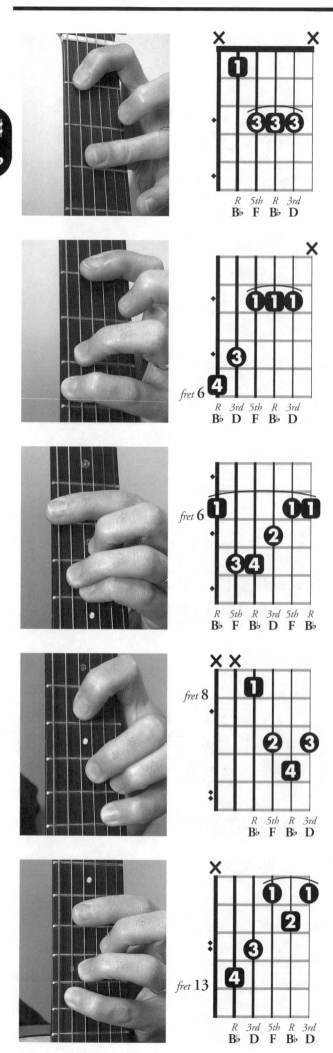

A♯
B♭

fret 6

R   5th R   3rd 5th R
B♭ F   B♭ D   F   B♭

R   3rd 5th R   3rd
B♭ D   F   B♭ D

fret 6

R   5th R   3rd
B♭ F   B♭ D

fret 8

R   3rd 5th R   3rd
B♭ D   F   B♭ D

fret 13

R   5th R   3rd
B♭ F   B♭ D

Bb6

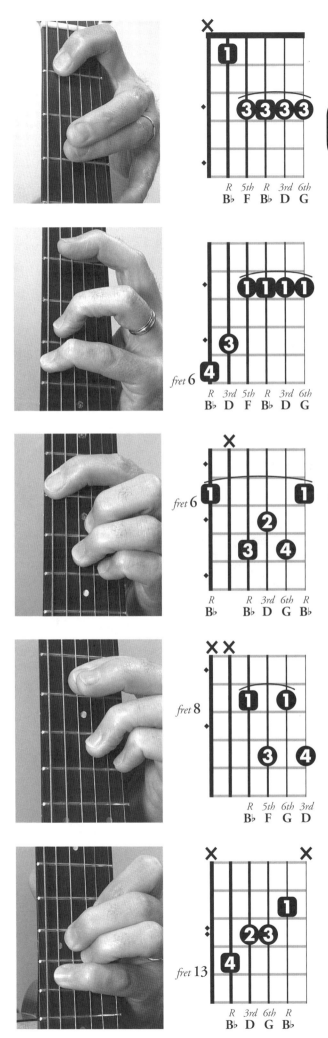

A#
Bb

R   5th R   3rd 6th
Bb F   Bb D   G

fret 6

R   3rd 5th R   3rd 6th
Bb D   F   Bb D   G

fret 6

R   R   3rd 6th R
Bb   Bb D   G   Bb

fret 8

R   5th 6th 3rd
Bb F   G   D

fret 13

R   3rd 6th R
Bb D   G   Bb

B♭maj7

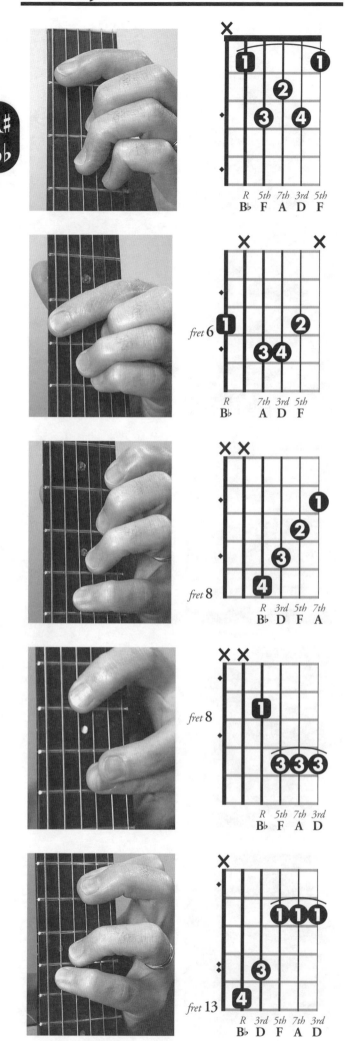

A#
B♭

R 5th 7th 3rd 5th
B♭ F A D F

fret 6

R 7th 3rd 5th
B♭ A D F

fret 8

R 3rd 5th 7th
B♭ D F A

fret 8

R 5th 7th 3rd
B♭ F A D

fret 13

R 3rd 5th 7th 3rd
B♭ D F A D

SCALE DEGREES: *R 3rd 5th 9th*
CHORD TONES: Bb D F C

Bb(9)

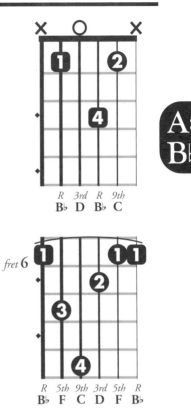

A#
Bb

R   3rd   R   9th
Bb   D   Bb   C

fret 6

R   5th   9th   3rd   5th   R
Bb   F   C   D   F   Bb

fret 13

R   3rd   5th   9th
Bb   D   F   C

SCALE DEGREES: *R 3rd 5th 7th 9th*
CHORD TONES: Bb D F A C

Bbmaj9

R   3rd   7th   9th
Bb   D   A   C

fret 6

R   3rd   7th   9th   5th   7th
Bb   D   A   C   F   A

B♭maj7(♯11)

SCALE DEGREES: *R 3rd 5th 7th ♯11th*
CHORD TONES: **B♭ D F A E**

R ♯11th 7th 3rd ♯11th
B♭ E A D E

fret 6

R   7th 3rd ♯11th
B♭   A D E

B♭6/9

SCALE DEGREES: *R 3rd 5th 6th 9th*
CHORD TONES: **B♭ D F G C**

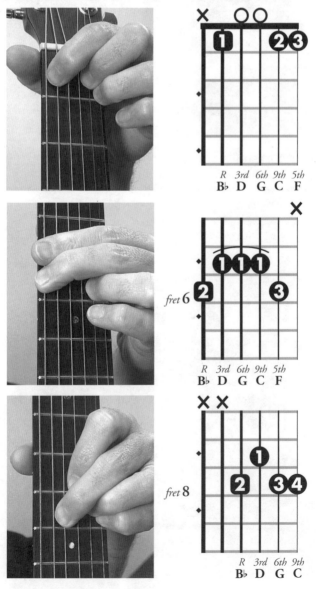

R 3rd 6th 9th 5th
B♭ D G C F

fret 6

R 3rd 6th 9th 5th
B♭ D G C F

fret 8

R 3rd 6th 9th
B♭ D G C

A♯
B♭

B♭sus2

A#
B♭

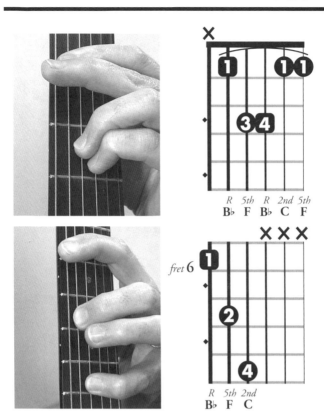

R	5th	R	2nd	5th
B♭	F	B♭	C	F

fret 6

R	5th	2nd
B♭	F	C

B♭sus4

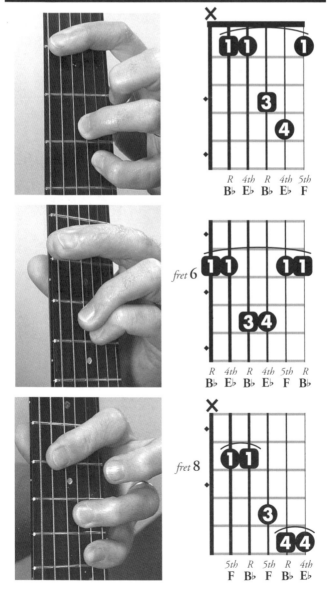

R	4th	R	4th	5th
B♭	E♭	B♭	E♭	F

fret 6

R	4th	R	4th	5th	R
B♭	E♭	B♭	E♭	F	B♭

fret 8

5th	R	5th	R	4th
F	B♭	F	B♭	E♭

The Ultimate Guitar Chord Casebook   39

B♭m

A#
B♭

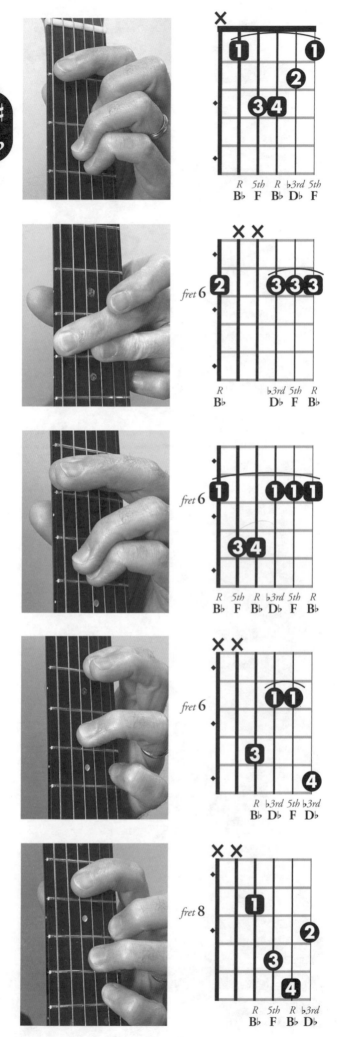

R 5th R ♭3rd 5th
B♭ F B♭ D♭ F

fret 6

R ♭3rd 5th R
B♭ D♭ F B♭

fret 6

R 5th R ♭3rd 5th R
B♭ F B♭ D♭ F B♭

fret 6

R ♭3rd 5th ♭3rd
B♭ D♭ F D♭

fret 8

R 5th R ♭3rd
B♭ F B♭ D♭

B♭m6

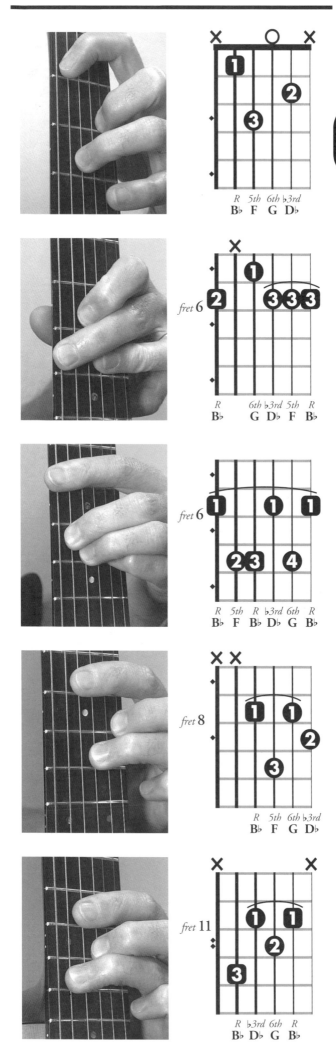

A#
B♭

R 5th 6th ♭3rd
B♭ F G D♭

fret 6

R 6th ♭3rd 5th R
B♭ G D♭ F B♭

fret 6

R 5th R ♭3rd 6th R
B♭ F B♭ D♭ G B♭

fret 8

R 5th 6th ♭3rd
B♭ F G D♭

fret 11

R ♭3rd 6th R
B♭ D♭ G B♭

B♭m7

A#
B♭

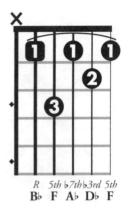

R 5th ♭7th ♭3rd 5th
B♭ F A♭ D♭ F

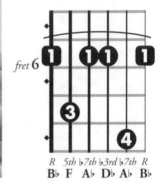

fret 6

R 5th ♭7th ♭3rd ♭7th R
B♭ F A♭ D♭ A♭ B♭

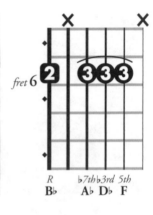

fret 6

R ♭7th ♭3rd 5th
B♭ A♭ D♭ F

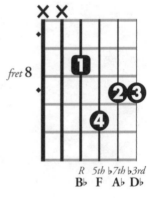

fret 8

R 5th ♭7th ♭3rd
B♭ F A♭ D♭

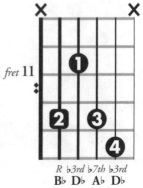

fret 11

R ♭3rd ♭7th ♭3rd
B♭ D♭ A♭ D♭

SCALE DEGREES: *R ♭3rd ♭5th ♭7th*
CHORD TONES: **B♭ D♭ F♭ A♭**

B♭m7(♭5)

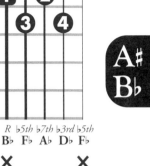

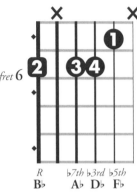

R ♭5th ♭7th ♭3rd ♭5th
B♭ F♭ A♭ D♭ F♭

fret 6

R ♭7th ♭3rd ♭5th
B♭ A♭ D♭ F♭

fret 8

R ♭5th ♭7th ♭3rd
B♭ F♭ A♭ D♭

SCALE DEGREES: *R ♭3rd 5th ♭7th 9th*
CHORD TONES: **B♭ D♭ F A♭ C**

B♭m9

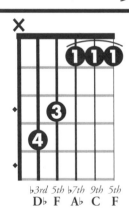

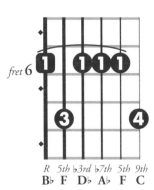

♭3rd 5th ♭7th 9th 5th
D♭ F A♭ C F

fret 6

R 5th ♭3rd ♭7th 5th 9th
B♭ F D♭ A♭ F C

B♭m(maj7)

SCALE DEGREES: R ♭3rd 5th 7th
CHORD TONES: B♭ D♭ F A

A#
B♭

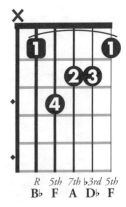

R	5th	7th	♭3rd	5th
B♭	F	A	D♭	F

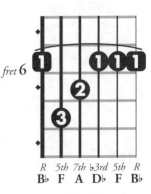

fret 6

R	5th	7th	♭3rd	5th	R
B♭	F	A	D♭	F	B♭

B♭m(9)

SCALE DEGREES: R ♭3rd 5th 9th
CHORD TONES: B♭ D♭ F C

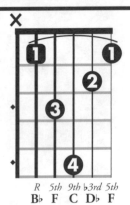

R	5th	9th	♭3rd	5th
B♭	F	C	D♭	F

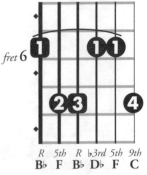

fret 6

R	5th	R	♭3rd	5th	9th
B♭	F	B♭	D♭	F	C

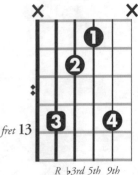

fret 13

R	♭3rd	5th	9th
B♭	D♭	F	C

SCALE DEGREES: *R ♭3rd 5th ♭7th 9th 11th*
CHORD TONES: **B♭ D♭ F A♭ C E♭**

B♭m11

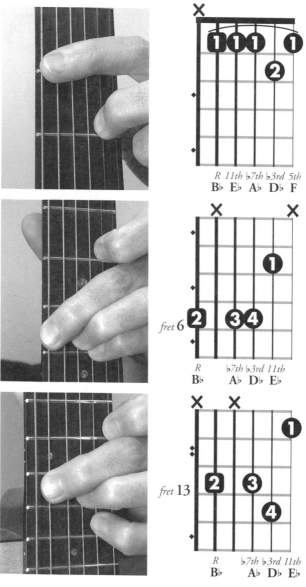

R 11th ♭7th ♭3rd 5th
B♭ E♭ A♭ D♭ F

R ♭7th ♭3rd 11th
B♭ A♭ D♭ E♭

fret 6

R ♭7th ♭3rd 11th
B♭ A♭ D♭ E♭

fret 13

SCALE DEGREES: *R ♭3rd 5th ♭7th 9th 11th 13th*
CHORD TONES: **B♭ D♭ F A♭ C E♭ G**

B♭m13

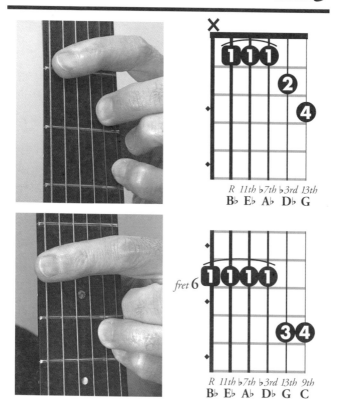

R 11th ♭7th ♭3rd 13th
B♭ E♭ A♭ D♭ G

fret 6

R 11th ♭7th ♭3rd 13th 9th
B♭ E♭ A♭ D♭ G C

B♭7

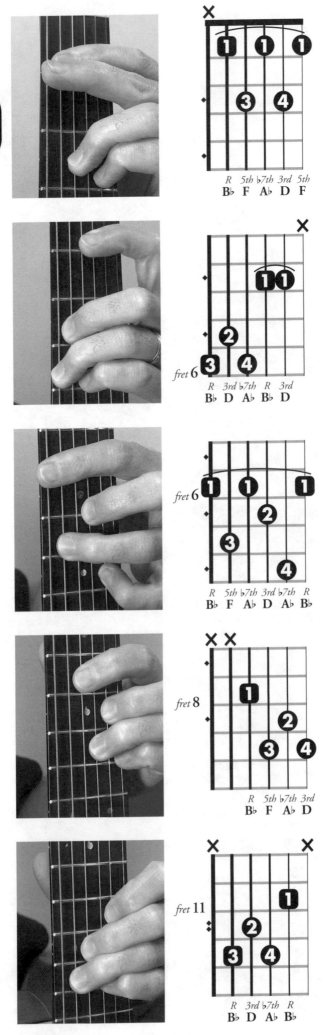

A#
B♭

R 5th ♭7th 3rd 5th
B♭ F A♭ D F

fret 6
R 3rd ♭7th R 3rd
B♭ D A♭ B♭ D

fret 6
R 5th ♭7th 3rd ♭7th R
B♭ F A♭ D A♭ B♭

fret 8
R 5th ♭7th 3rd
B♭ F A♭ D

fret 11
R 3rd ♭7th R
B♭ D A♭ B♭

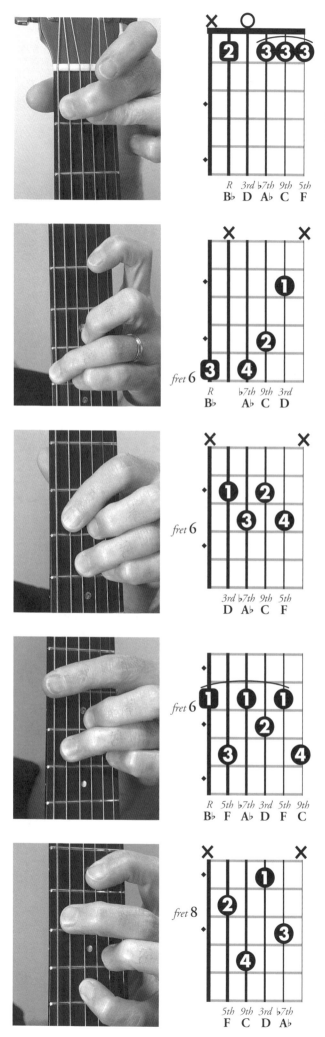

The Ultimate Guitar Chord Casebook 47

B♭7sus4

A♯
B♭

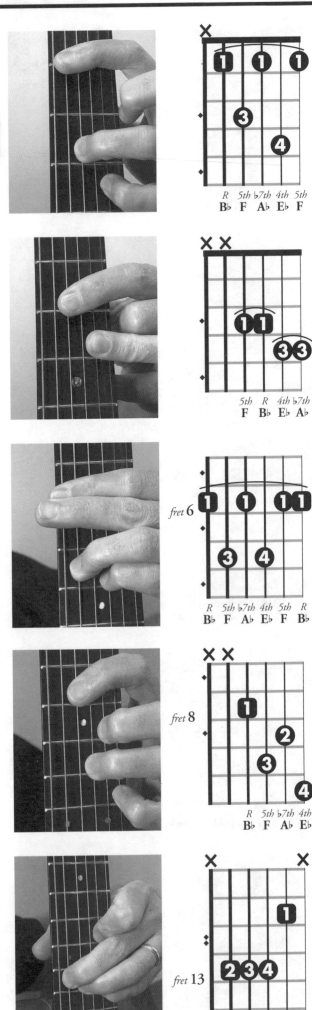

R   5th ♭7th 4th 5th
B♭ F   A♭   E♭   F

5th R   4th ♭7th
F   B♭ E♭   A♭

fret 6

R   5th ♭7th 4th 5th R
B♭ F   A♭   E♭   F   B♭

fret 8

R   5th ♭7th 4th
B♭ F   A♭   E♭

fret 13

R   4th ♭7th R
B♭ E♭   A♭   B♭

SCALE DEGREES: *R 4th 5th ♭7th 9th*
CHORD TONES: **B♭ E♭ F A♭ C**

B♭9sus4

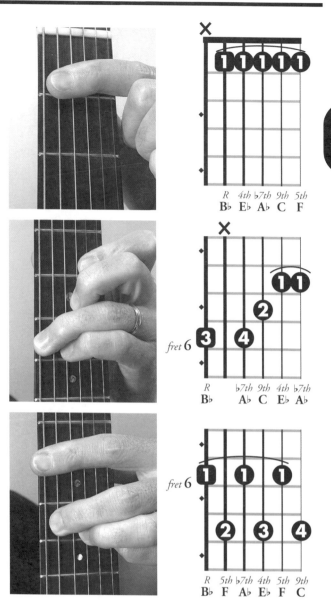

A#
B♭

R 4th ♭7th 9th 5th
B♭ E♭ A♭ C F

fret 6

R ♭7th 9th 4th ♭7th
B♭ A♭ C E♭ A♭

fret 6

R 5th ♭7th 4th 5th 9th
B♭ F A♭ E♭ F C

SCALE DEGREES: *R 3rd 5th ♭7th 9th 11th 13th*
CHORD TONES: **B♭ D F A♭ C E♭ G**

B♭13

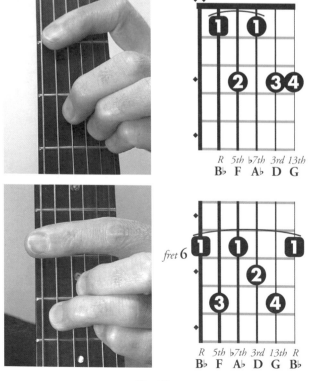

R 5th ♭7th 3rd 13th
B♭ F A♭ D G

fret 6

R 5th ♭7th 3rd 13th R
B♭ F A♭ D G B♭

B♭7(♭5)

R ♭5th ♭7th 3rd
B♭ F♭ A♭ D

fret 6

R ♭7th 3rd ♭5th
B♭ A♭ D F♭

B♭7(♯5)

SCALE DEGREES: *R 3rd ♯5th ♭7th*
CHORD TONES: **B♭ D F♯ A♭**

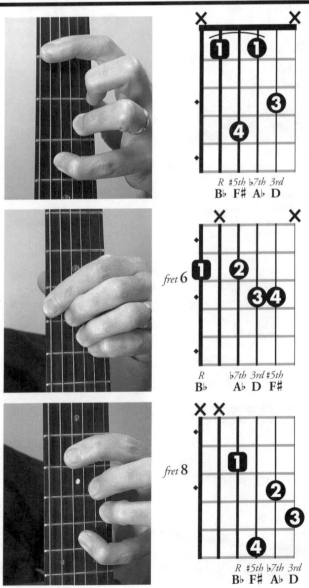

R ♯5th ♭7th 3rd
B♭ F♯ A♭ D

fret 6

R ♭7th 3rd ♯5th
B♭ A♭ D F♯

fret 8

R ♯5th ♭7th 3rd
B♭ F♯ A♭ D

A♯
B♭

SCALE DEGREES: *R 3rd 5th ♭7th ♭9th*
CHORD TONES: B♭ D F A♭ C♭

B♭7(♭9)

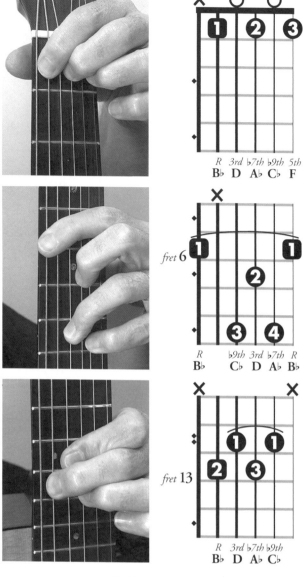

R   3rd ♭7th ♭9th 5th
B♭ D   A♭   C♭   F

fret 6

R   ♭9th 3rd ♭7th R
B♭   C♭   D   A♭   B♭

fret 13

R   3rd ♭7th ♭9th
B♭ D   A♭   C♭

SCALE DEGREES: *R 3rd 5th ♭7th #9th*
CHORD TONES: B♭ D F A♭ C#

B♭7(#9)

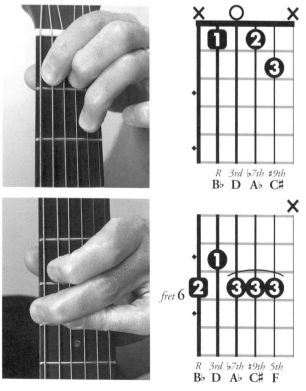

R   3rd ♭7th #9th
B♭ D   A♭   C#

fret 6

R   3rd ♭7th #9th 5th
B♭ D   A♭   C#   F

B♭9(♭5)

SCALE DEGREES: R 3rd ♭5th ♭7th 9th
CHORD TONES: B♭ D F♭ A♭ C

R 3rd ♭7th 9th ♭5th
B♭ D A♭ C F♭

fret 6

R 3rd ♭7th 9th ♭5th
B♭ D A♭ C F♭

B♭9(#5)

SCALE DEGREES: R 3rd #5th ♭7th 9th
CHORD TONES: B♭ D F# A♭ C

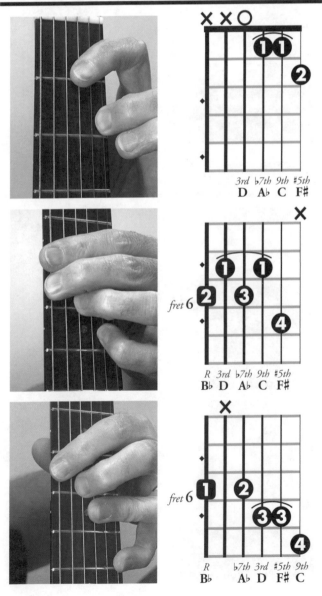

3rd ♭7th 9th #5th
D A♭ C F#

fret 6

R 3rd ♭7th 9th #5th
B♭ D A♭ C F#

fret 6

R ♭7th 3rd #5th 9th
B♭ A♭ D F# C

A#
B♭

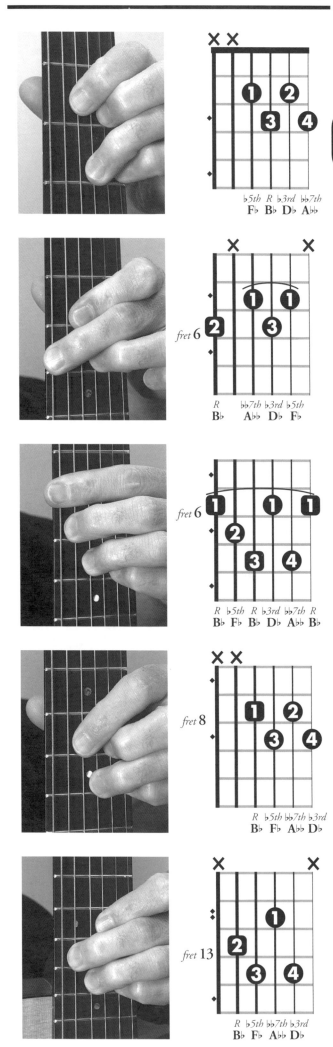

SCALE DEGREES: R ♭3rd ♭5th ♭♭7th
CHORD TONES: B♭ D♭ F♭ A♭♭

B♭dim7

A#
B♭

♭5th R ♭3rd ♭♭7th
F♭ B♭ D♭ A♭♭

fret 6

R ♭♭7th ♭3rd ♭5th
B♭ A♭♭ D♭ F♭

fret 6

R ♭5th R ♭3rd ♭♭7th R
B♭ F♭ B♭ D♭ A♭♭ B♭

fret 8

R ♭5th ♭♭7th ♭3rd
B♭ F♭ A♭♭ D♭

fret 13

R ♭5th ♭♭7th ♭3rd
B♭ F♭ A♭♭ D♭

SCALE DEGREES: R 3rd 5th
CHORD TONES: B D# F#

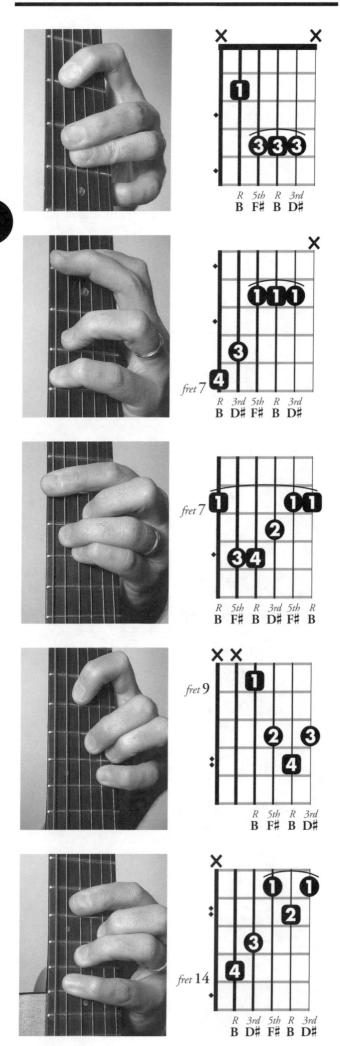

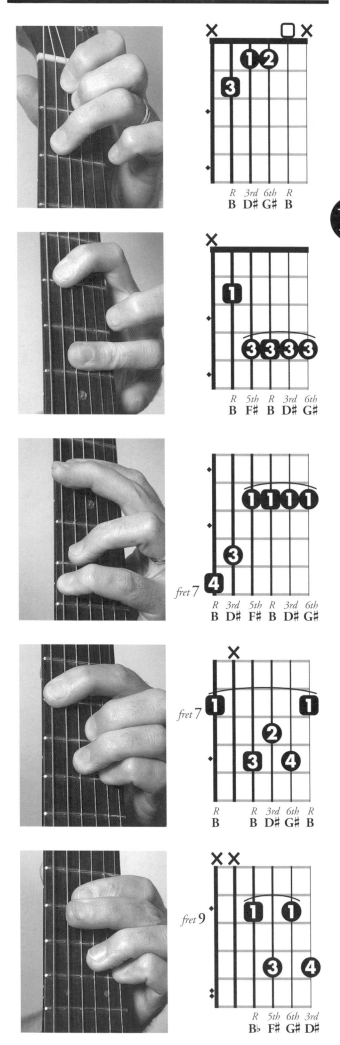

Bmaj7

B

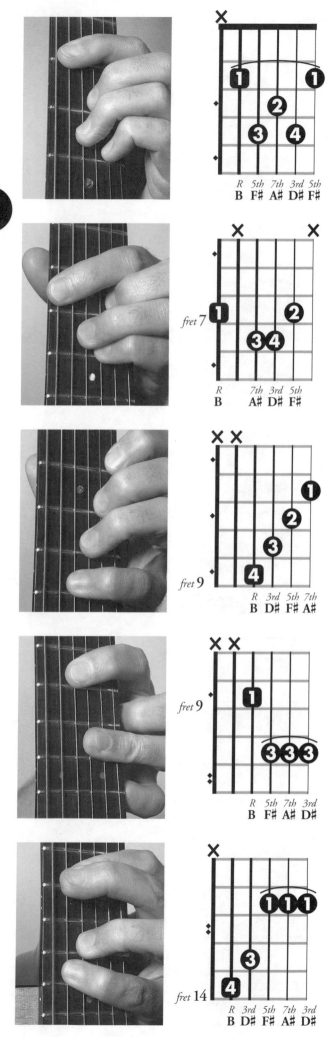

R   5th   7th   3rd 5th
B   F#   A#   D#   F#

fret 7

R   7th   3rd 5th
B   A#   D#   F#

fret 9

R   3rd   5th   7th
B   D#   F#   A#

fret 9

R   5th   7th   3rd
B   F#   A#   D#

fret 14

R   3rd   5th   7th   3rd
B   D#   F#   A#   D#

SCALE DEGREES: *R   3rd   5th   9th*
CHORD TONES: B   D#   F#   C#

B(9)

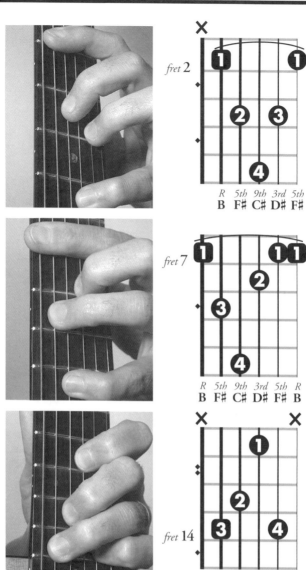

fret 2

R   5th   9th   3rd   5th
B   F#   C#   D#   F#

fret 7

R   5th   9th   3rd   5th   R
B   F#   C#   D#   F#   B

fret 14

R   3rd   5th   9th
B   D#   F#   C#

SCALE DEGREES: *R   3rd   5th   7th   9th*
CHORD TONES: B   D#   F#   A#   C#

Bmaj9

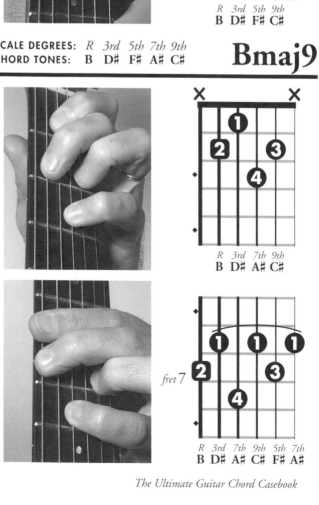

R   3rd   7th   9th
B   D#   A#   C#

fret 7

R   3rd   7th   9th   5th   7th
B   D#   A#   C#   F#   A#

Bmaj7(#11)

SCALE DEGREES: *R 3rd 5th 7th #11th*
CHORD TONES: B D# F# A# E#

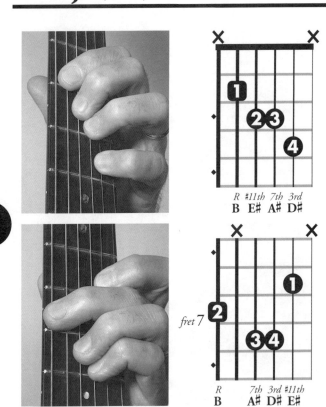

R #11th 7th 3rd
B E# A# D#

fret 7

R   7th 3rd #11th
B   A#   D#   E#

B6/9

SCALE DEGREES: *R 3rd 5th 6th 9th*
CHORD TONES: B D# F# G# C#

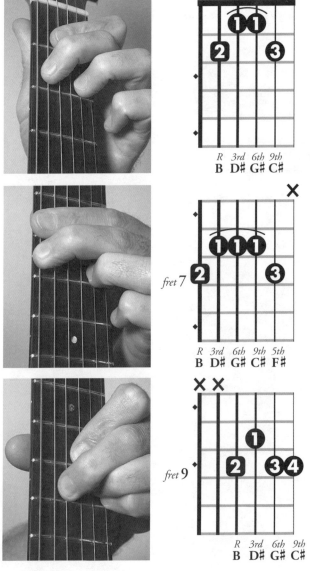

R   3rd 6th 9th
B   D#   G#   C#

fret 7

R   3rd 6th 9th 5th
B   D#   G#   C#   F#

fret 9

R   3rd 6th 9th
B   D#   G#   C#

Bsus2

R   5th R   2nd 5th
B   F#   B   C#   F#

B

fret 7

R   5th 2nd
B   F#   C#

Bsus4

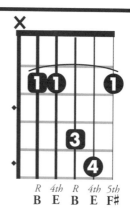

R   4th R   4th 5th
B   E   B   E   F#

fret 7

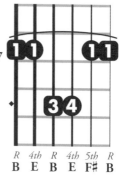

R   4th R   4th 5th R
B   E   B   E   F#   B

fret 9

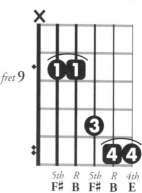

5th R   5th R   4th
F#   B   F#   B   E

Bm

×

R *5th* *R* *♭3rd* *5th*
B **F♯** **B** **D** **F♯**

× ×

fret 7

R *♭3rd* *5th* *R*
B **D** **F♯** **B**

fret 7

R *5th* *R* *♭3rd* *5th* *R*
B **F♯** **B** **D** **F♯** **B**

× ×

fret 7

R *♭3rd* *5th* *♭3rd*
B **D** **F♯** **D**

× ×

fret 9

R *5th* *R* *♭3rd*
B **F♯** **B** **D**

B

Bm6

B

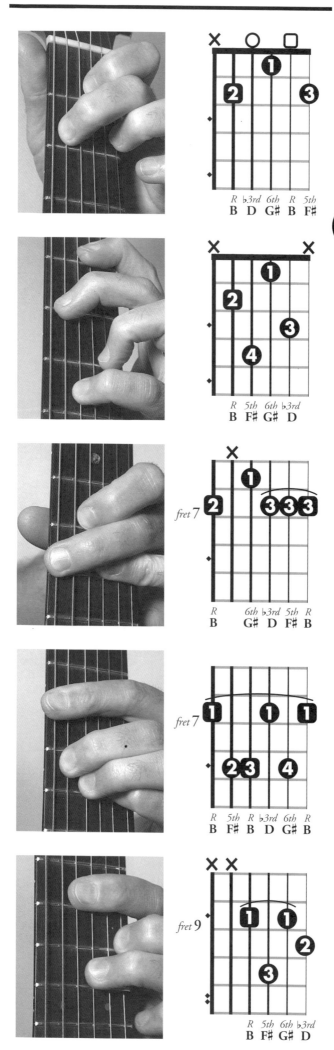

R	*♭3rd*	*6th*	*R*	*5th*
B	D	G♯	B	F♯

R	*5th*	*6th*	*♭3rd*
B	F♯	G♯	D

fret 7

R		*6th*	*♭3rd*	*5th*	*R*
B		G♯	D	F♯	B

fret 7

R	*5th*	*R*	*♭3rd*	*6th*	*R*
B	F♯	B	D	G♯	B

fret 9

R	*5th*	*6th*	*♭3rd*
B	F♯	G♯	D

Bm7

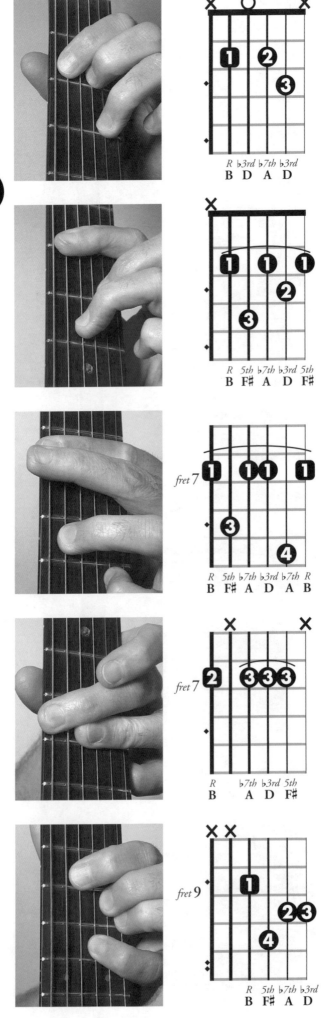

R ♭3rd ♭7th ♭3rd
B D A D

R 5th ♭7th ♭3rd 5th
B F# A D F#

fret 7

R 5th ♭7th ♭3rd ♭7th R
B F# A D A B

fret 7

R ♭7th ♭3rd 5th
B A D F#

fret 9

R 5th ♭7th ♭3rd
B F# A D

SCALE DEGREES: *R ♭3rd ♭5th ♭7th*
CHORD TONES: B D F A

Bm7(♭5)

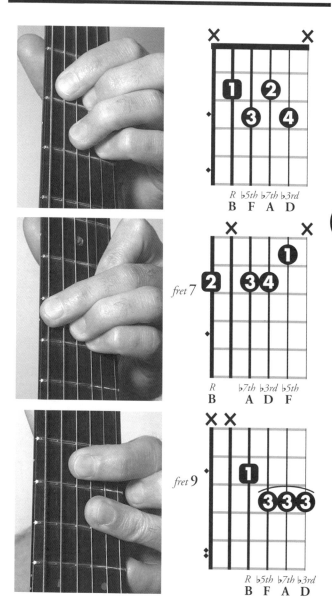

R ♭5th ♭7th ♭3rd
B F A D

R ♭7th ♭3rd ♭5th
B A D F

R ♭5th ♭7th ♭3rd
B F A D

SCALE DEGREES: *R ♭3rd 5th ♭7th 9th*
CHORD TONES: B D F♯ A C♯

Bm9

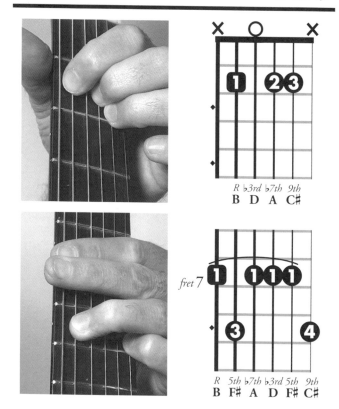

R ♭3rd ♭7th 9th
B D A C♯

R 5th ♭7th ♭3rd 5th 9th
B F♯ A D F♯ C♯

Bm(maj7)

SCALE DEGREES: R ♭3rd 5th 7th
CHORD TONES: B D F# A#

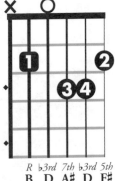

R	♭3rd	7th	♭3rd	5th
B	D	A#	D	F#

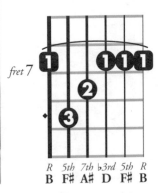

fret 7

R	5th	7th	♭3rd	5th	R
B	F#	A#	D	F#	B

Bm(9)

SCALE DEGREES: R ♭3rd 5th 9th
CHORD TONES: B D F# C#

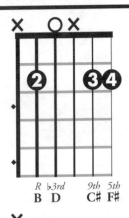

R	♭3rd		9th	5th
B	D		C#	F#

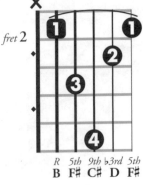

fret 2

R	5th	9th	♭3rd	5th
B	F#	C#	D	F#

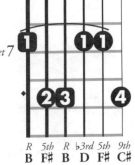

fret 7

R	5th	R	♭3rd	5th	9th
B	F#	B	D	F#	C#

B

SCALE DEGREES: *R ♭3rd 5th ♭7th 9th 11th*
CHORD TONES: B D F# A C# E

Bm11

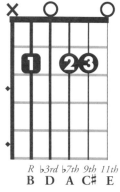

R ♭3rd ♭7th 9th 11th
B D A C# E

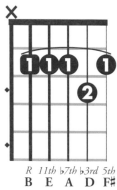

R 11th ♭7th ♭3rd 5th
B E A D F#

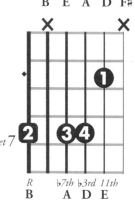

fret 7

R ♭7th ♭3rd 11th
B A D E

SCALE DEGREES: *R ♭3rd 5th ♭7th 9th 11th 13th*
CHORD TONES: B D F# A C# E G#

Bm13

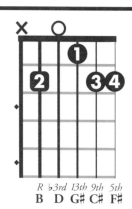

R ♭3rd 13th 9th 5th
B D G# C# F#

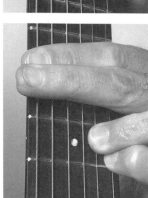

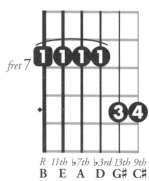

fret 7

R 11th ♭7th ♭3rd 13th 9th
B E A D G# C#

B7

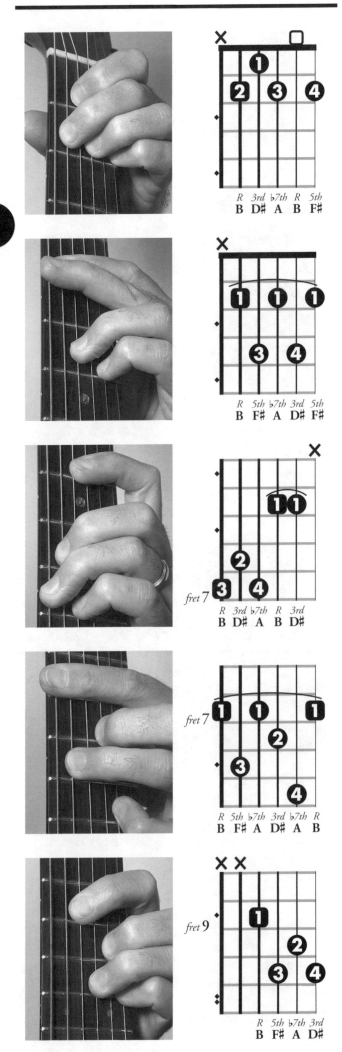

B

R 3rd ♭7th R 5th
B D♯ A B F♯

R 5th ♭7th 3rd 5th
B F♯ A D♯ F♯

fret 7
R 3rd ♭7th R 3rd
B D♯ A B D♯

fret 7
R 5th ♭7th 3rd ♭7th R
B F♯ A D♯ A B

fret 9
R 5th ♭7th 3rd
B F♯ A D♯

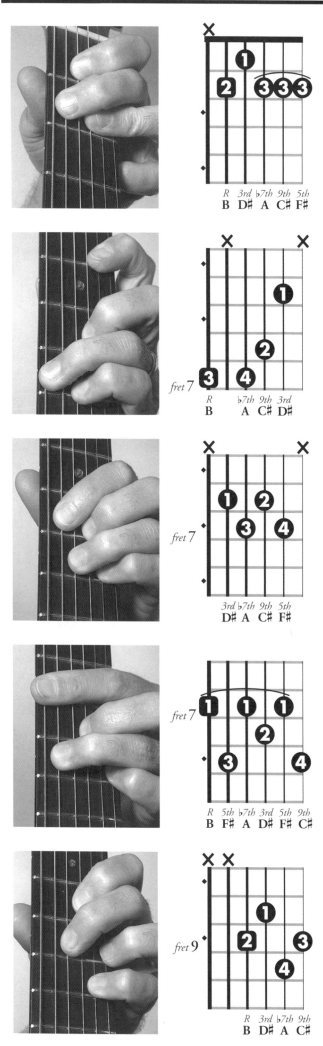

B7sus4

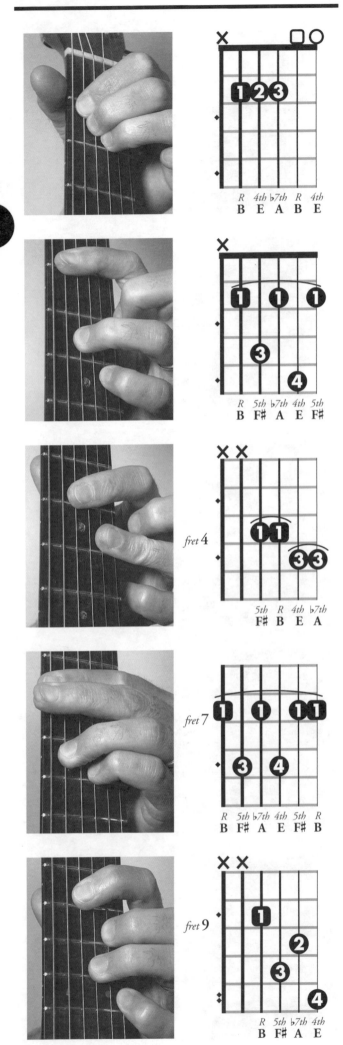

R 4th ♭7th R 4th
B E A B E

R 5th ♭7th 4th 5th
B F# A E F#

fret 4

5th R 4th ♭7th
F# B E A

fret 7

R 5th ♭7th 4th 5th R
B F# A E F# B

fret 9

R 5th ♭7th 4th
B F# A E

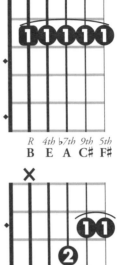

B

R   4th ♭7th 9th 5th
B   E   A   C# F#

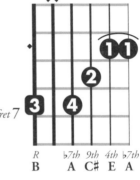

fret 7

R   ♭7th 9th 4th ♭7th
B   A   C#   E   A

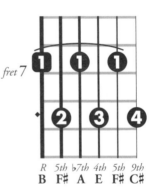

fret 7

R   5th ♭7th 4th 5th 9th
B   F#   A   E   F#   C#

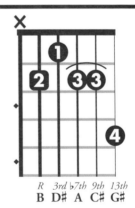

R   3rd ♭7th 9th 13th
B   D#   A   C#   G#

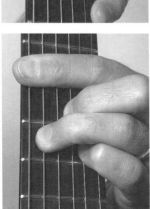

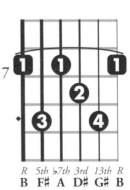

fret 7

R   5th ♭7th 3rd 13th R
B   F#   A   D#   G#   B

B7(♭5)

SCALE DEGREES: *R 3rd ♭5th ♭7th*
CHORD TONES: B D# F A

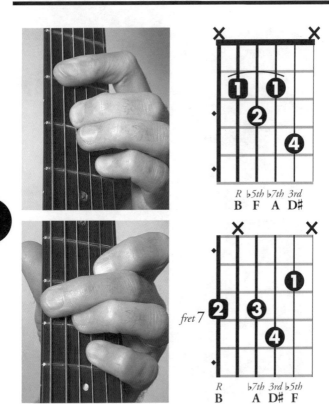

R ♭5th ♭7th 3rd
B F A D#

fret 7

R ♭7th 3rd ♭5th
B A D# F

B7(#5)

SCALE DEGREES: *R 3rd #5th ♭7th*
CHORD TONES: B D# F## A

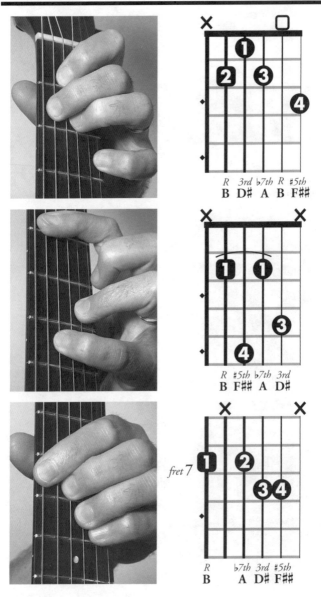

R 3rd ♭7th R #5th
B D# A B F##

R #5th ♭7th 3rd
B F## A D#

fret 7

R ♭7th 3rd #5th
B A D# F##

SCALE DEGREES: *R   3rd 5th ♭7th ♭9th*
CHORD TONES: B D♯ F♯ A C

B7(♭9)

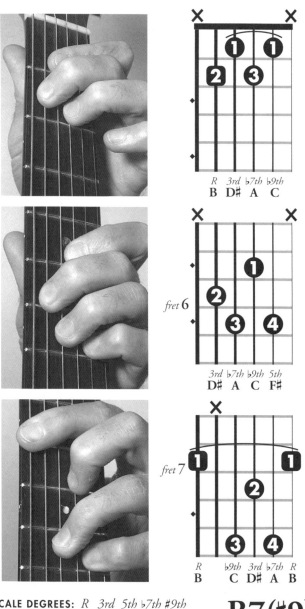

R   3rd ♭7th ♭9th
B D♯ A C

fret 6

3rd ♭7th ♭9th 5th
D♯ A C F♯

fret 7

R   ♭9th 3rd ♭7th R
B C D♯ A B

SCALE DEGREES: *R   3rd 5th ♭7th ♯9th*
CHORD TONES: B D♯ F♯ A C♯♯

B7(♯9)

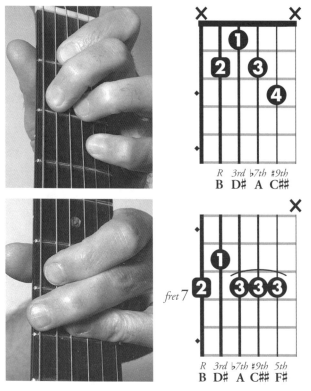

R   3rd ♭7th ♯9th
B D♯ A C♯♯

fret 7

R   3rd ♭7th ♯9th 5th
B D♯ A C♯♯ F♯

B9(♭5)

SCALE DEGREES: R 3rd ♭5th ♭7th 9th
CHORD TONES: B D# F A C#

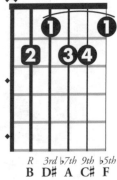

R   3rd ♭7th 9th ♭5th
B   D#   A   C#   F

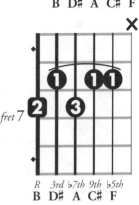

fret 7

R   3rd ♭7th 9th ♭5th
B   D#   A   C#   F

B9(#5)

SCALE DEGREES: R 3rd #5th ♭7th 9th
CHORD TONES: B D# F## A C#

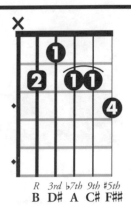

R   3rd ♭7th 9th #5th
B   D#   A   C#   F##

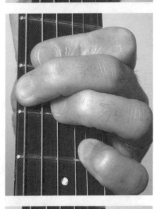

fret 7

R   3rd ♭7th 9th #5th
B   D#   A   C#   F##

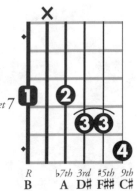

fret 7

R   ♭7th 3rd #5th 9th
B   A   D#   F##   C#

B

Bdim7

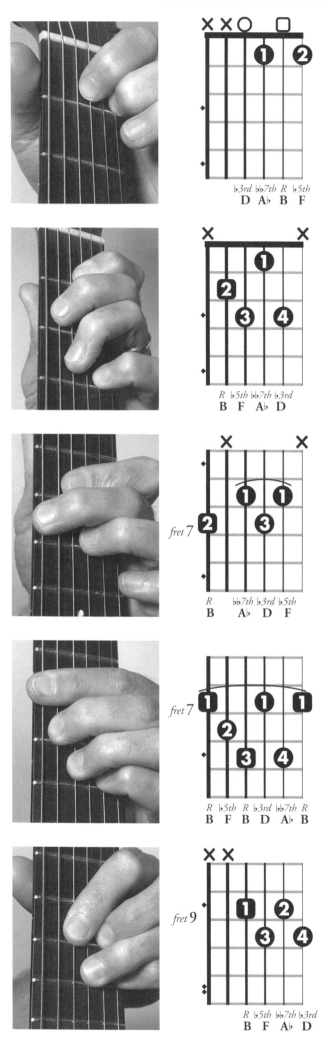

B

♭3rd ♭♭7th R ♭5th
D A♭ B F

R ♭5th ♭♭7th ♭3rd
B F A♭ D

fret 7

R   ♭♭7th ♭3rd ♭5th
B   A♭   D   F

fret 7

R ♭5th R ♭3rd ♭♭7th R
B F B D A♭ B

fret 9

R ♭5th ♭♭7th ♭3rd
B F A♭ D

C

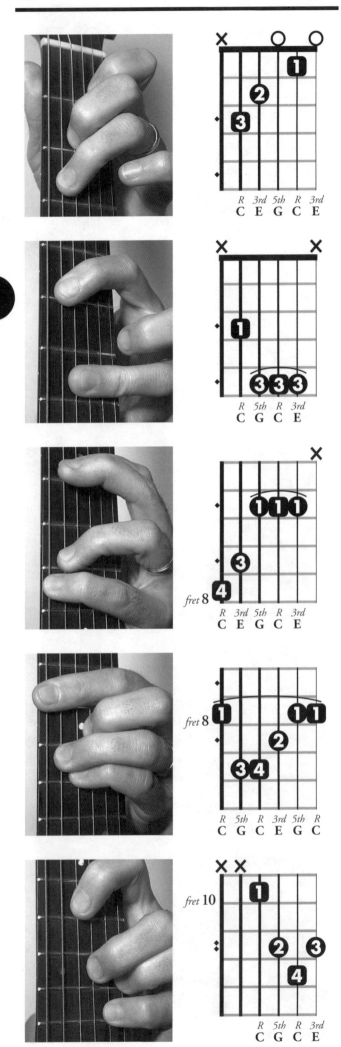

R   3rd 5th R   3rd
C   E   G   C   E

R   5th R   3rd
C   G   C   E

fret 8

R   3rd 5th R   3rd
C   E   G   C   E

fret 8

R   5th R   3rd 5th R
C   G   C   E   G   C

fret 10

R   5th R   3rd
C   G   C   E

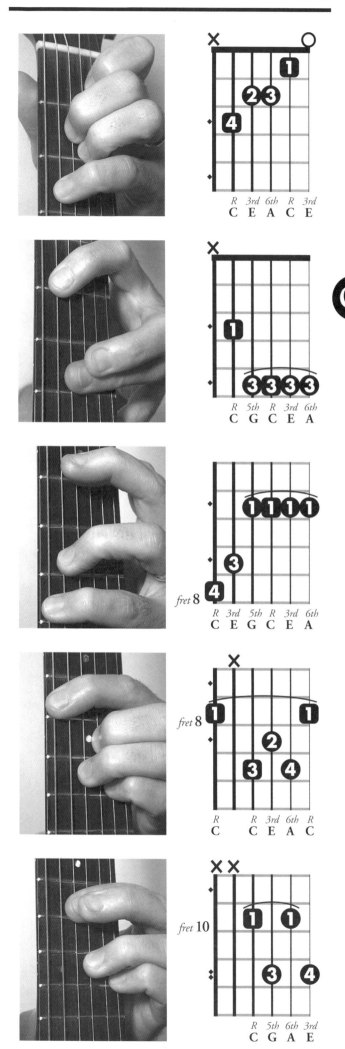

Cmaj7

SCALE DEGREES: R 3rd 5th 7th
CHORD TONES: C E G B

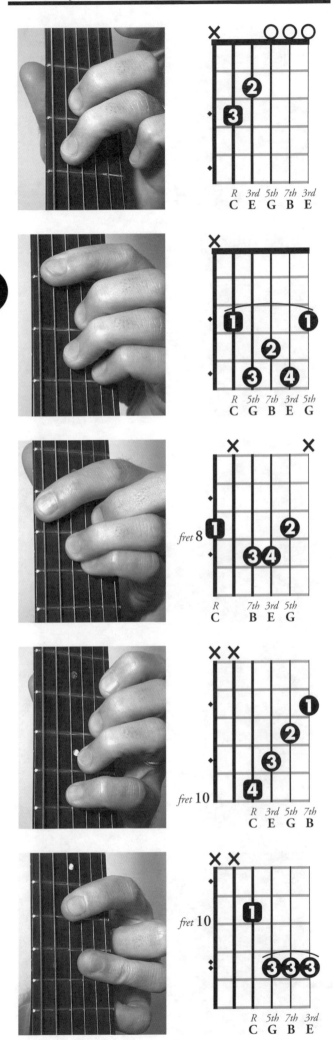

R   3rd 5th 7th 3rd
C   E   G   B   E

R   5th 7th 3rd 5th
C   G   B   E   G

fret 8

R   7th 3rd 5th
C   B   E   G

fret 10

R   3rd 5th 7th
C   E   G   B

fret 10

R   5th 7th 3rd
C   G   B   E

SCALE DEGREES: *R 3rd 5th 9th*
CHORD TONES: C E G D

C(9)

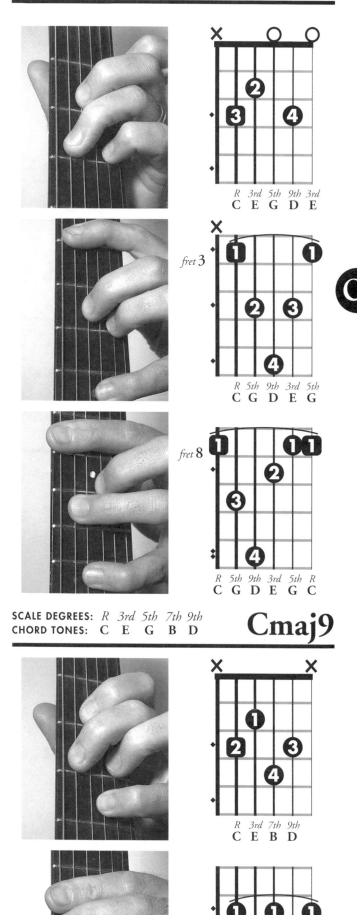

R   3rd 5th 9th 3rd
C   E   G   D   E

fret 3

R   5th 9th 3rd 5th
C   G   D   E   G

fret 8

R   5th 9th 3rd 5th R
C   G   D   E   G   C

SCALE DEGREES: *R 3rd 5th 7th 9th*
CHORD TONES: C E G B D

Cmaj9

R   3rd 7th 9th
C   E   B   D

fret 8

R   3rd 7th 9th 5th 7th
C   E   B   D   G   B

C

Cmaj7(#11)

SCALE DEGREES: R 3rd 5th 7th #11th
CHORD TONES: C E G B F#

C6/9

SCALE DEGREES: R 3rd 5th 6th 9th
CHORD TONES: C E G A D

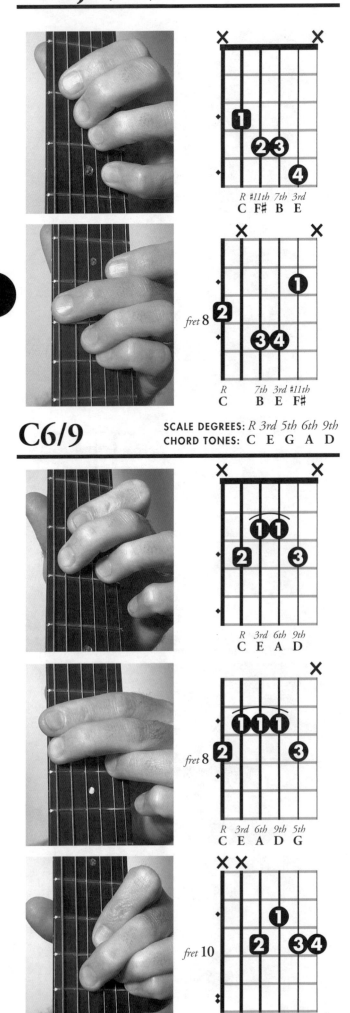

Csus2

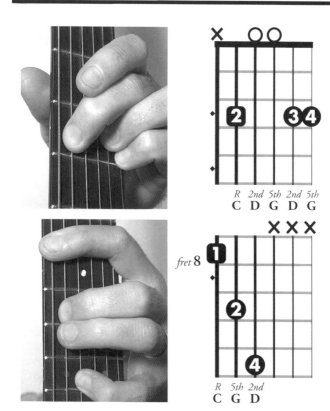

R	2nd	5th	2nd	5th
C	D	G	D	G

fret 8

R	5th	2nd
C	G	D

Csus4

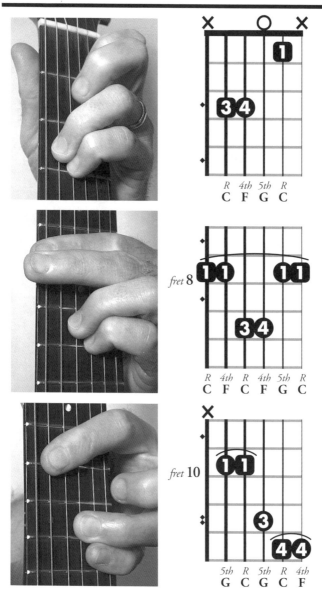

R	4th	5th	R
C	F	G	C

fret 8

R	4th	R	4th	5th	R
C	F	C	F	G	C

fret 10

5th	R	5th	R	4th
G	C	G	C	F

Cm

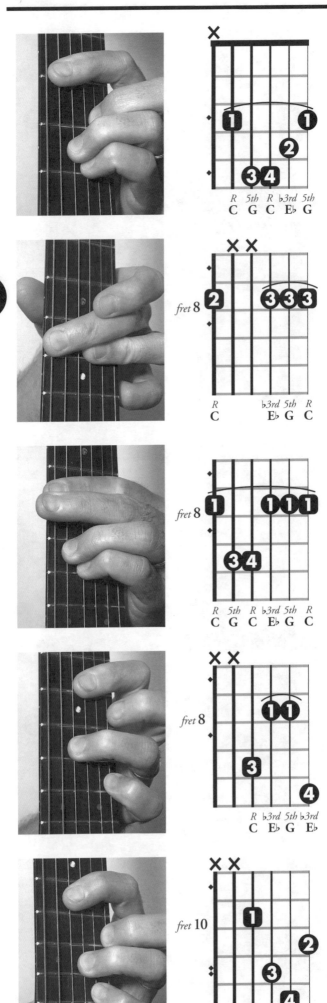

R	5th	R	♭3rd	5th
C	G	C	E♭	G

fret 8

R			♭3rd	5th	R
C			E♭	G	C

fret 8

R	5th	R	♭3rd	5th	R
C	G	C	E♭	G	C

fret 8

R	♭3rd	5th	♭3rd
C	E♭	G	E♭

fret 10

R	5th	R	♭3rd
C	G	C	E♭

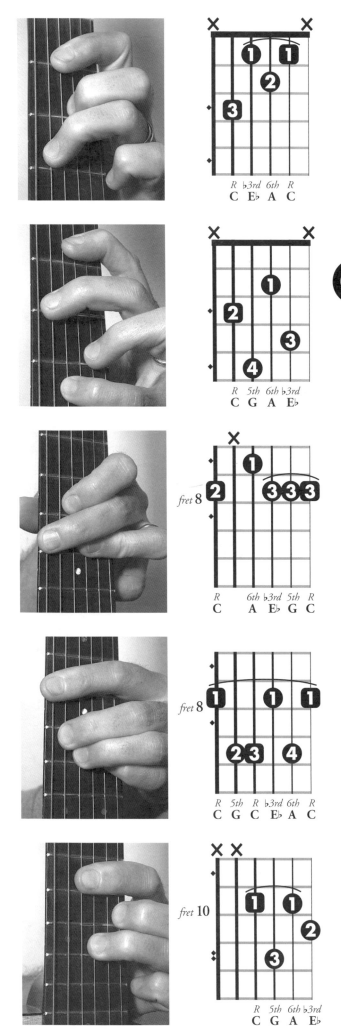

SCALE DEGREES: R ♭3rd 5th 6th
CHORD TONES: C E♭ G A

Cm6

C

R ♭3rd 6th R
C E♭ A C

R 5th 6th ♭3rd
C G A E♭

fret 8

R 6th ♭3rd 5th R
C A E♭ G C

fret 8

R 5th R ♭3rd 6th R
C G C E♭ A C

fret 10

R 5th 6th ♭3rd
C G A E♭

Cm7

SCALE DEGREES: R ♭3rd 5th ♭7th
CHORD TONES: C E♭ G B♭

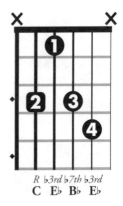

R ♭3rd ♭7th ♭3rd
C E♭ B♭ E♭

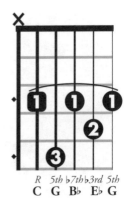

R 5th ♭7th ♭3rd 5th
C G B♭ E♭ G

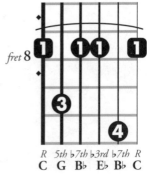

fret 8

R 5th ♭7th ♭3rd ♭7th R
C G B♭ E♭ B♭ C

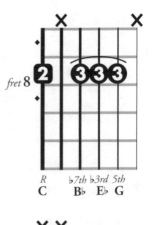

fret 8

R ♭7th ♭3rd 5th
C B♭ E♭ G

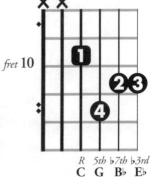

fret 10

R 5th ♭7th ♭3rd
C G B♭ E♭

C

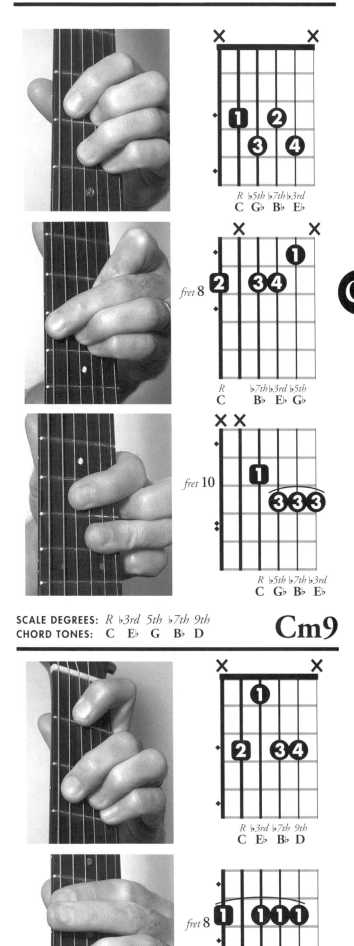

C

R ♭5th ♭7th ♭3rd
C G♭ B♭ E♭

fret 8

R ♭7th ♭3rd ♭5th
C   B♭ E♭ G♭

fret 10

R ♭5th ♭7th ♭3rd
C G♭ B♭ E♭

R ♭3rd ♭7th 9th
C E♭ B♭ D

fret 8

R 5th ♭7th ♭3rd 5th 9th
C G B♭ E♭ G D

Cm(maj7)

SCALE DEGREES: R ♭3rd 5th 7th
CHORD TONES: C E♭ G B

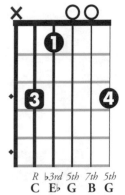

R ♭3rd 5th 7th 5th
C E♭ G B G

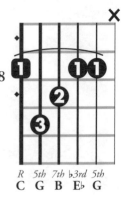

fret 8

R 5th 7th ♭3rd 5th
C G B E♭ G

Cm(9)

SCALE DEGREES: R ♭3rd 5th 9th
CHORD TONES: C E♭ G D

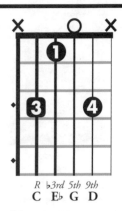

R ♭3rd 5th 9th
C E♭ G D

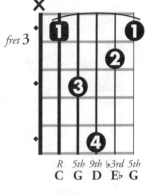

fret 3

R 5th 9th ♭3rd 5th
C G D E♭ G

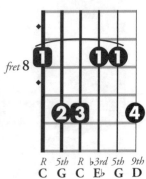

fret 8

R 5th R ♭3rd 5th 9th
C G C E♭ G D

SCALE DEGREES: *R ♭3rd 5th ♭7th 9th 11th*
CHORD TONES: C E♭ G B♭ D F

Cm11

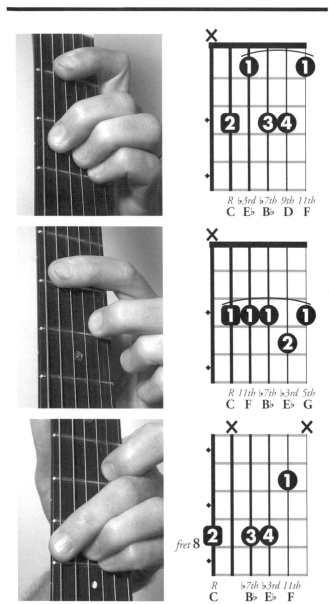

R ♭3rd ♭7th 9th 11th
C E♭ B♭ D F

R 11th ♭7th ♭3rd 5th
C F B♭ E♭ G

fret 8

R ♭7th ♭3rd 11th
C B♭ E♭ F

SCALE DEGREES: *R ♭3rd 5th ♭7th 9th 11th 13th*
CHORD TONES: C E♭ G B♭ D F A

Cm13

R 11th ♭7th ♭3rd 13th
C F B♭ E♭ A

fret 8

R 11th ♭7th ♭3rd 13th 9th
C F B♭ E♭ A D

C7

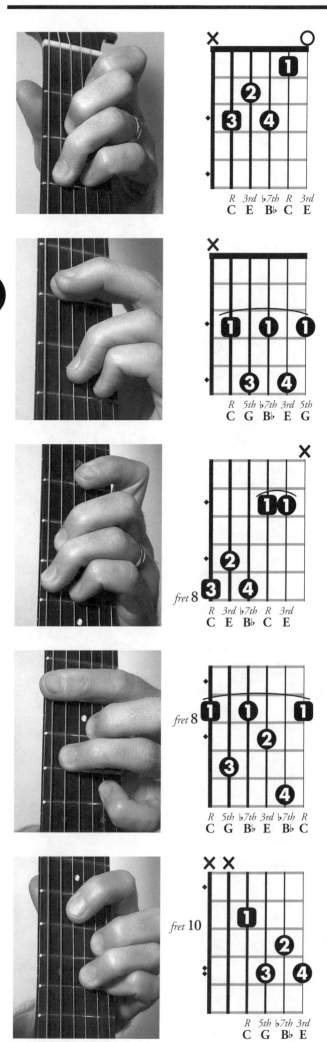

R 3rd ♭7th R 3rd
C E B♭ C E

R 5th ♭7th 3rd 5th
C G B♭ E G

fret 8

R 3rd ♭7th R 3rd
C E B♭ C E

fret 8

R 5th ♭7th 3rd ♭7th R
C G B♭ E B♭ C

fret 10

R 5th ♭7th 3rd
C G B♭ E

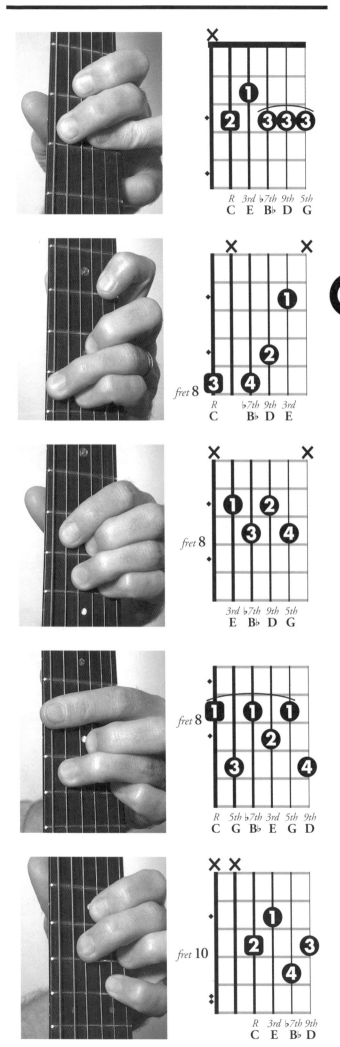

C

First diagram:
R   3rd ♭7th 9th   5th
C   E   B♭   D   G

Second diagram (fret 8):
R   ♭7th 9th 3rd
C   B♭   D   E

Third diagram (fret 8):
3rd ♭7th 9th 5th
E   B♭   D   G

Fourth diagram (fret 8):
R   5th ♭7th 3rd 5th 9th
C   G   B♭   E   G   D

Fifth diagram (fret 10):
R   3rd ♭7th 9th
C   E   B♭   D

C7sus4

SCALE DEGREES: R 4th 5th ♭7th
CHORD TONES: C F G B♭

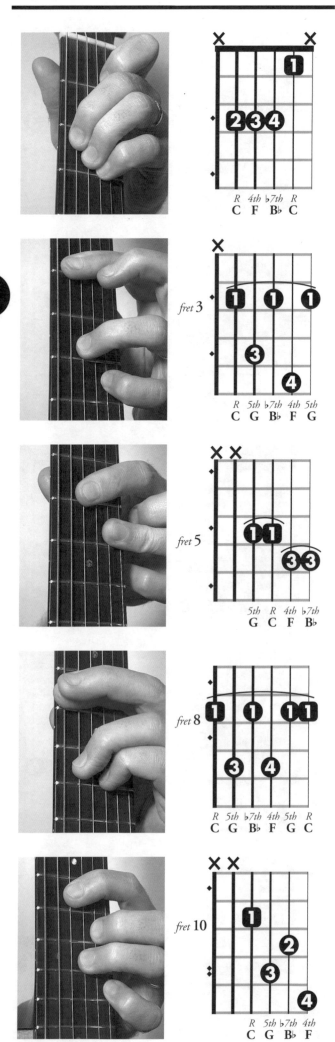

R 4th ♭7th R
C   F   B♭   C

fret 3

R 5th ♭7th 4th 5th
C   G   B♭   F   G

fret 5

5th R 4th ♭7th
 G   C   F   B♭

fret 8

R 5th ♭7th 4th 5th R
C   G   B♭   F   G   C

fret 10

R 5th ♭7th 4th
C   G   B♭   F

SCALE DEGREES: *R 4th 5th ♭7th 9th*
CHORD TONES: C F G B♭ D

C9sus4

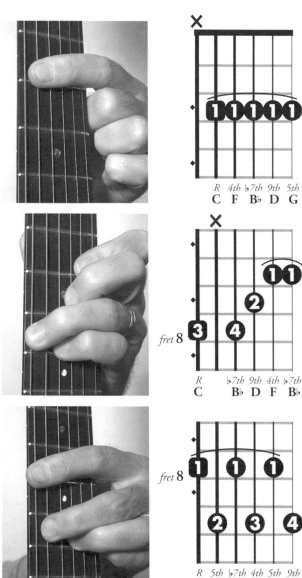

R   4th ♭7th 9th 5th
C   F   B♭   D   G

fret 8

R   ♭7th 9th 4th ♭7th
C   B♭   D   F   B♭

fret 8

R   5th ♭7th 4th 5th 9th
C   G   B♭   F   G   D

SCALE DEGREES: *R 3rd 5th ♭7th 9th 11th 13th*
CHORD TONES: C E G B♭ D F A

C13

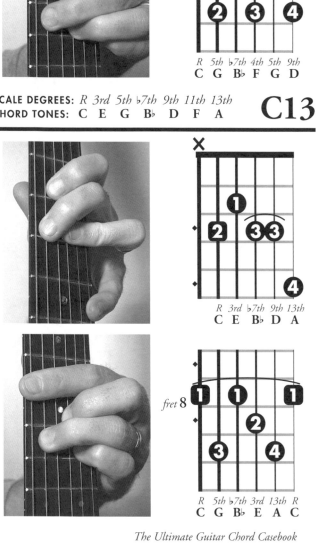

R   3rd ♭7th 9th 13th
C   E   B♭   D   A

fret 8

R   5th ♭7th 3rd 13th R
C   G   B♭   E   A   C

C7(♭5)

SCALE DEGREES: R 3rd ♭5th ♭7th
CHORD TONES: C E G♭ B♭

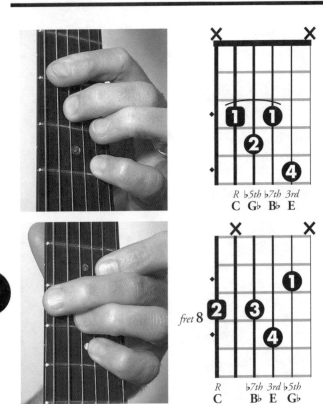

R ♭5th ♭7th 3rd
C G♭ B♭ E

fret 8

R ♭7th 3rd ♭5th
C B♭ E G♭

C7(♯5)

SCALE DEGREES: R 3rd ♯5th ♭7th
CHORD TONES: C E G♯ B♭

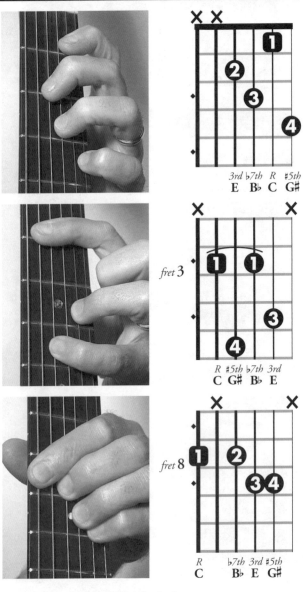

3rd ♭7th R ♯5th
E B♭ C G♯

fret 3

R ♯5th ♭7th 3rd
C G♯ B♭ E

fret 8

R ♭7th 3rd ♯5th
C B♭ E G♯

SCALE DEGREES: *R   3rd   5th   ♭7th   ♭9th*
CHORD TONES: C   E   G   B♭   D♭

C7(♭9)

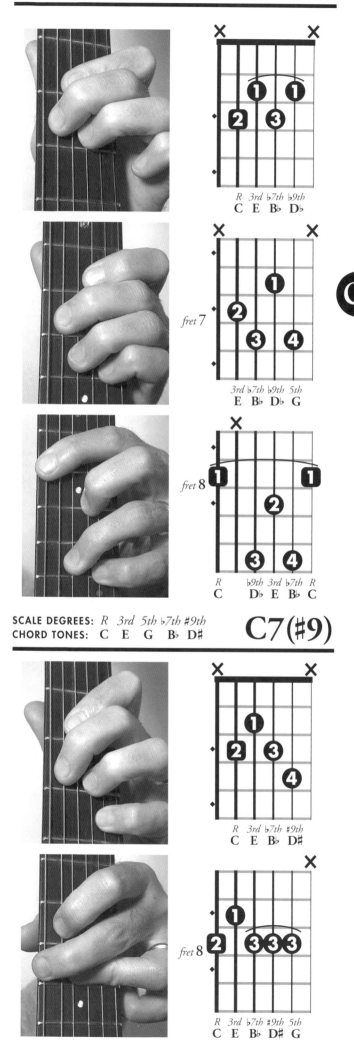

R   3rd   ♭7th   ♭9th
C   E   B♭   D♭

fret 7

3rd   ♭7th   ♭9th   5th
E   B♭   D♭   G

fret 8

R   ♭9th   3rd   ♭7th   R
C   D♭   E   B♭   C

C

SCALE DEGREES: *R   3rd   5th   ♭7th   ♯9th*
CHORD TONES: C   E   G   B♭   D♯

C7(♯9)

R   3rd   ♭7th   ♯9th
C   E   B♭   D♯

fret 8

R   3rd   ♭7th   ♯9th   5th
C   E   B♭   D♯   G

C9(♭5)

SCALE DEGREES: R 3rd ♭5th ♭7th 9th
CHORD TONES: C E G♭ B♭ D

R 3rd ♭7th 9th ♭5th
C E B♭ D G♭

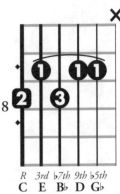

fret 8

R 3rd ♭7th 9th ♭5th
C E B♭ D G♭

C9(♯5)

SCALE DEGREES: R 3rd ♯5th ♭7th 9th
CHORD TONES: C E G♯ B♭ D

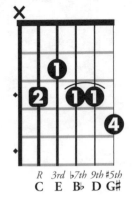

R 3rd ♭7th 9th ♯5th
C E B♭ D G♯

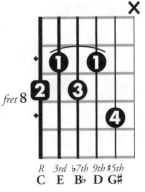

fret 8

R 3rd ♭7th 9th ♯5th
C E B♭ D G♯

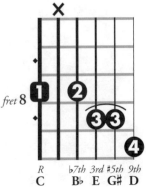

fret 8

R   ♭7th 3rd ♯5th 9th
C   B♭ E G♯ D

Cdim7

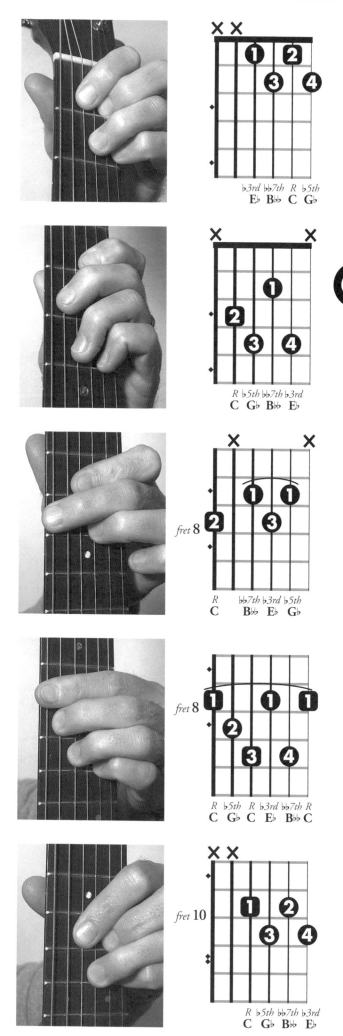

♭3rd ♭♭7th R ♭5th
E♭ B♭♭ C G♭

R ♭5th ♭♭7th ♭3rd
C G♭ B♭♭ E♭

fret 8

R ♭♭7th ♭3rd ♭5th
C B♭♭ E♭ G♭

fret 8

R ♭5th R ♭3rd ♭♭7th R
C G♭ C E♭ B♭♭ C

fret 10

R ♭5th ♭♭7th ♭3rd
C G♭ B♭♭ E♭

C

D♭

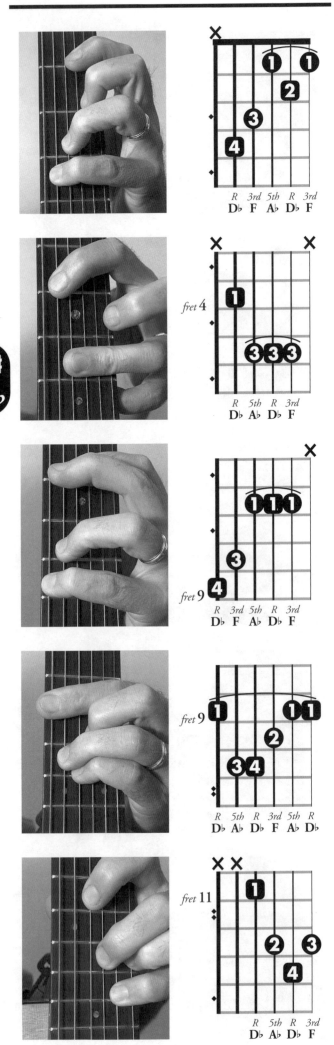

C#
D♭

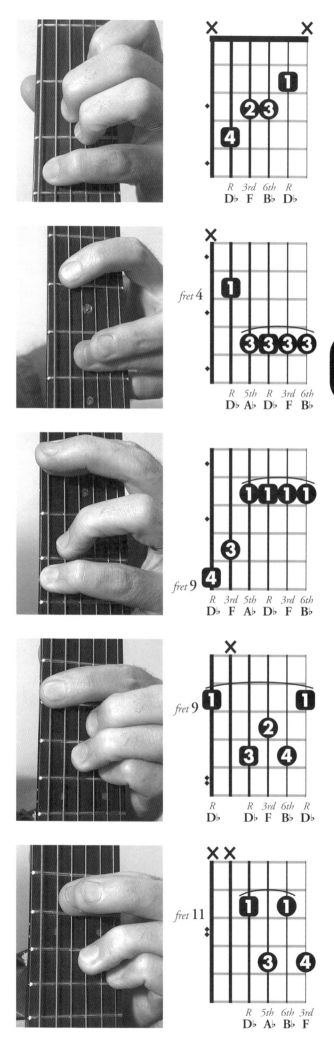

C♯ D♭

D♭maj7

SCALE DEGREES: R 3rd 5th 7th
CHORD TONES: D♭ F A♭ C

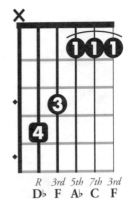

R 3rd 5th 7th 3rd
D♭ F A♭ C F

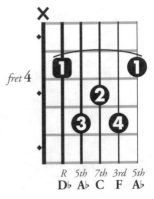

fret 4

R 5th 7th 3rd 5th
D♭ A♭ C F A♭

C#
D♭

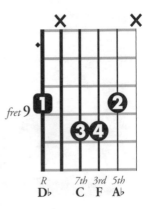

fret 9

R 7th 3rd 5th
D♭ C F A♭

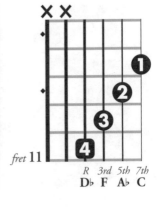

fret 11

R 3rd 5th 7th
D♭ F A♭ C

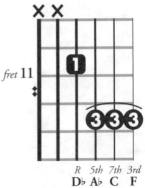

fret 11

R 5th 7th 3rd
D♭ A♭ C F

SCALE DEGREES: *R   3rd   5th   9th*
CHORD TONES: **D♭   F   A♭   E♭**

D♭(9)

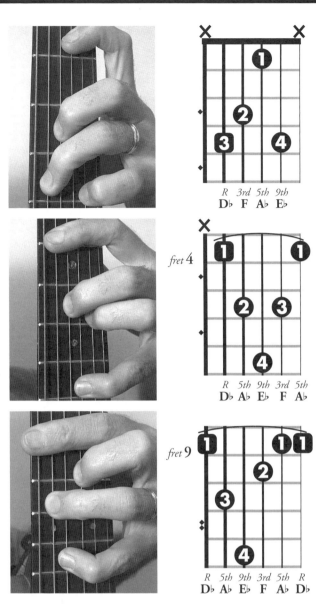

×   ×

R   3rd   5th   9th
D♭   F   A♭   E♭

fret 4

R   5th   9th   3rd   5th
D♭   A♭   E♭   F   A♭

fret 9

R   5th   9th   3rd   5th   R
D♭   A♭   E♭   F   A♭   D♭

C♯
D♭

SCALE DEGREES: *R   3rd   5th   7th   9th*
CHORD TONES: **D♭   F   A♭   C   E♭**

D♭maj9

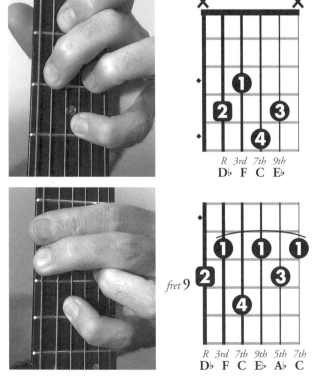

×   ×

R   3rd   7th   9th
D♭   F   C   E♭

fret 9

R   3rd   7th   9th   5th   7th
D♭   F   C   E♭   A♭   C

D♭maj7(#11)

SCALE DEGREES: *R 3rd 5th 7th #11th*
CHORD TONES: D♭ F A♭ C G

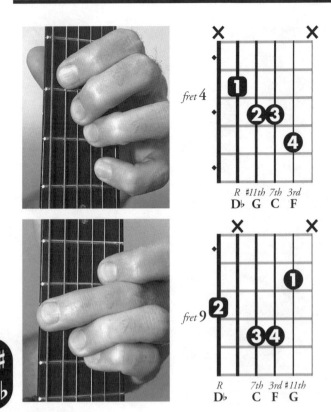

fret 4

R	#11th	7th	3rd
D♭	G	C	F

fret 9

R		7th	3rd	#11th
D♭		C	F	G

D♭6/9

SCALE DEGREES: *R 3rd 5th 6th 9th*
CHORD TONES: D♭ F A♭ B♭ E♭

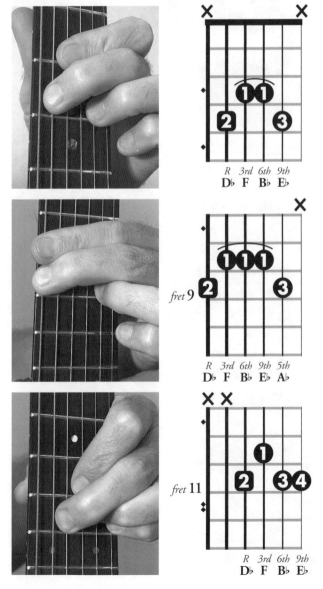

R	3rd	6th	9th
D♭	F	B♭	E♭

fret 9

R	3rd	6th	9th	5th
D♭	F	B♭	E♭	A♭

fret 11

R	3rd	6th	9th
D♭	F	B♭	E♭

C♯ / D♭

SCALE DEGREES: *R   2nd 5th*
CHORD TONES: **D♭   E♭   A♭**

D♭sus2

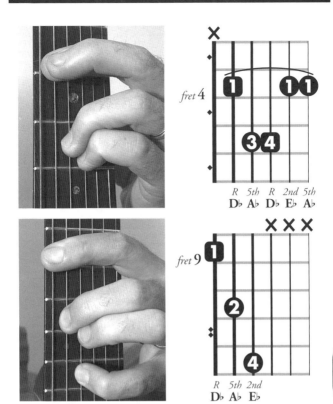

fret 4

R	5th	R	2nd	5th
D♭	**A♭**	**D♭**	**E♭**	**A♭**

fret 9

R	5th	2nd
D♭	**A♭**	**E♭**

C♯
D♭

SCALE DEGREES: *R   4th 5th*
CHORD TONES: **D♭   G♭   A♭**

D♭sus4

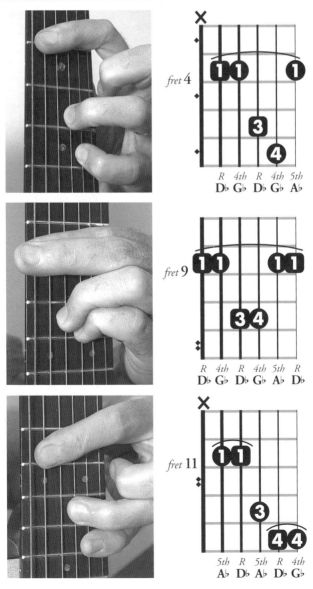

fret 4

R	4th	R	4th	5th
D♭	**G♭**	**D♭**	**G♭**	**A♭**

fret 9

R	4th	R	4th	5th	R
D♭	**G♭**	**D♭**	**G♭**	**A♭**	**D♭**

fret 11

5th	R	5th	R	4th
A♭	**D♭**	**A♭**	**D♭**	**G♭**

D♭m

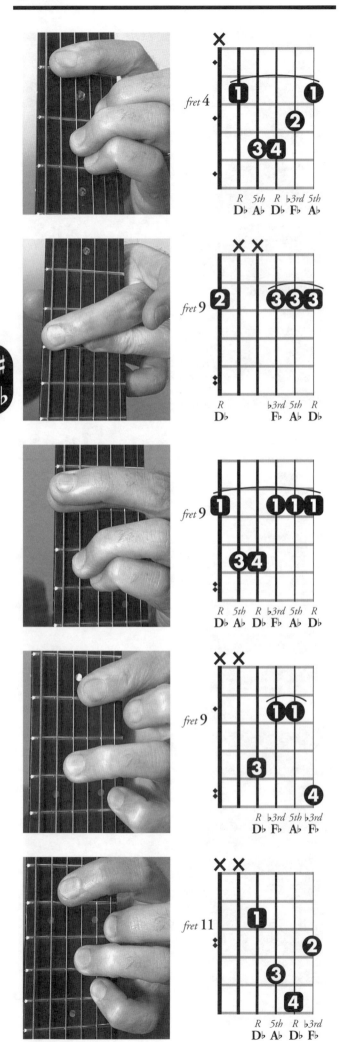

SCALE DEGREES: *R ♭3rd 5th*
CHORD TONES: **D♭ F♭ A♭**

C#
D♭

fret 4

R 5th R ♭3rd 5th
D♭ A♭ D♭ F♭ A♭

fret 9

R ♭3rd 5th R
D♭ F♭ A♭ D♭

fret 9

R 5th R ♭3rd 5th R
D♭ A♭ D♭ F♭ A♭ D♭

fret 9

R ♭3rd 5th ♭3rd
D♭ F♭ A♭ F♭

fret 11

R 5th R ♭3rd
D♭ A♭ D♭ F♭

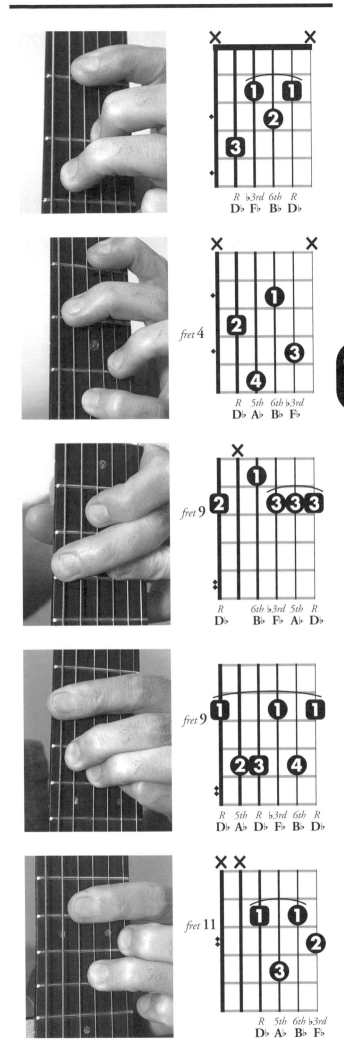

D♭m7

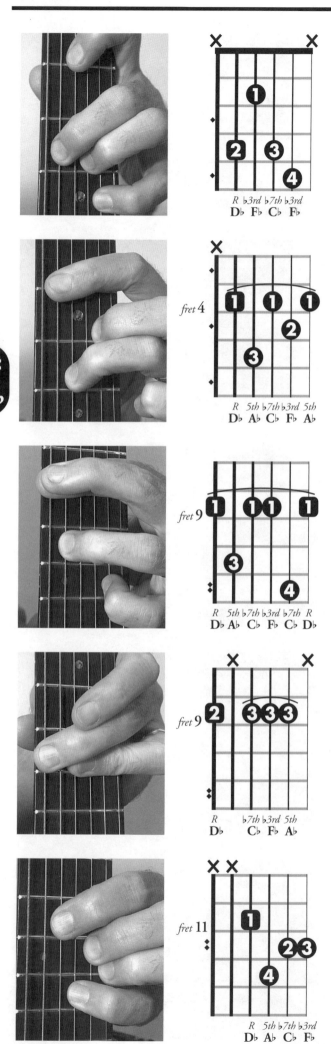

SCALE DEGREES: R ♭3rd 5th ♭7th
CHORD TONES: D♭ F♭ A♭ C♭

C#
D♭

R ♭3rd ♭7th ♭3rd
D♭ F♭ C♭ F♭

fret 4

R 5th ♭7th ♭3rd 5th
D♭ A♭ C♭ F♭ A♭

fret 9

R 5th ♭7th ♭3rd ♭7th R
D♭ A♭ C♭ F♭ C♭ D♭

fret 9

R ♭7th ♭3rd 5th
D♭ C♭ F♭ A♭

fret 11

R 5th ♭7th ♭3rd
D♭ A♭ C♭ F♭

SCALE DEGREES: R ♭3rd ♭5th ♭7th
CHORD TONES: D♭ F♭ A♭♭ C♭

D♭m7(♭5)

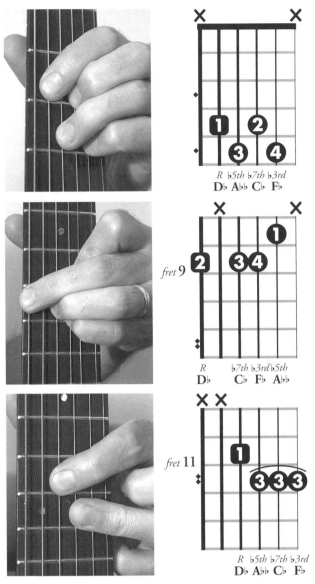

R ♭5th ♭7th ♭3rd
D♭ A♭♭ C♭ F♭

fret 9

R ♭7th ♭3rd ♭5th
D♭ C♭ F♭ A♭♭

C#
D♭

fret 11

R ♭5th ♭7th ♭3rd
D♭ A♭♭ C♭ F♭

SCALE DEGREES: R ♭3rd 5th ♭7th 9th
CHORD TONES: D♭ F♭ A♭ C♭ E♭

D♭m9

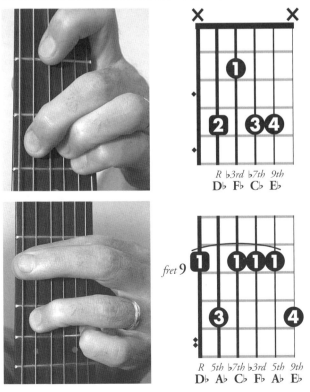

R ♭3rd ♭7th 9th
D♭ F♭ C♭ E♭

fret 9

R 5th ♭7th ♭3rd 5th 9th
D♭ A♭ C♭ F♭ A♭ E♭

D♭m(maj7)

SCALE DEGREES: R ♭3rd 5th 7th
CHORD TONES: D♭ F♭ A♭ C

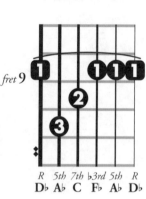

fret 4

R 5th 7th ♭3rd
D♭ A♭ C F♭

fret 9

R 5th 7th ♭3rd 5th R
D♭ A♭ C F♭ A♭ D♭

C#
D♭

D♭m(9)

SCALE DEGREES: R ♭3rd 5th 9th
CHORD TONES: D♭ F♭ A♭ E♭

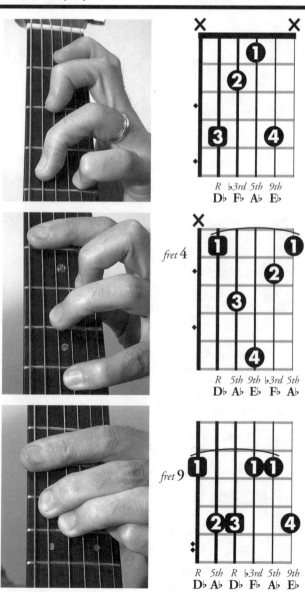

R ♭3rd 5th 9th
D♭ F♭ A♭ E♭

fret 4

R 5th 9th ♭3rd 5th
D♭ A♭ E♭ F♭ A♭

fret 9

R 5th R ♭3rd 5th 9th
D♭ A♭ D♭ F♭ A♭ E♭

SCALE DEGREES: *R ♭3rd 5th ♭7th 9th 11th*
CHORD TONES: D♭ F♭ A♭ C♭ E♭ G♭

D♭m11

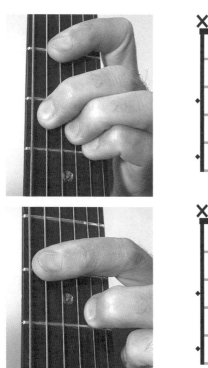

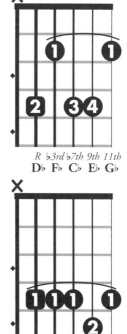

R ♭3rd ♭7th 9th 11th
D♭ F♭ C♭ E♭ G♭

C♯
D♭

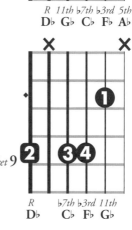

R 11th ♭7th ♭3rd 5th
D♭ G♭ C♭ F♭ A♭

fret 9

R ♭7th ♭3rd 11th
D♭ C♭ F♭ G♭

SCALE DEGREES: *R ♭3rd 5th ♭7th 9th 11th 13th*
CHORD TONES: D♭ F♭ A♭ C♭ E♭ G♭ B♭

D♭m13

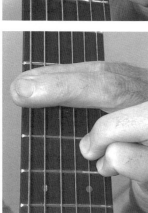

fret 4

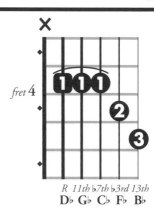

R 11th ♭7th ♭3rd 13th
D♭ G♭ C♭ F♭ B♭

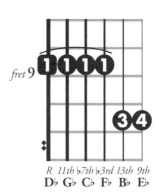

fret 9

R 11th ♭7th ♭3rd 13th 9th
D♭ G♭ C♭ F♭ B♭ E♭

The Ultimate Guitar Chord Casebook   105

D♭7

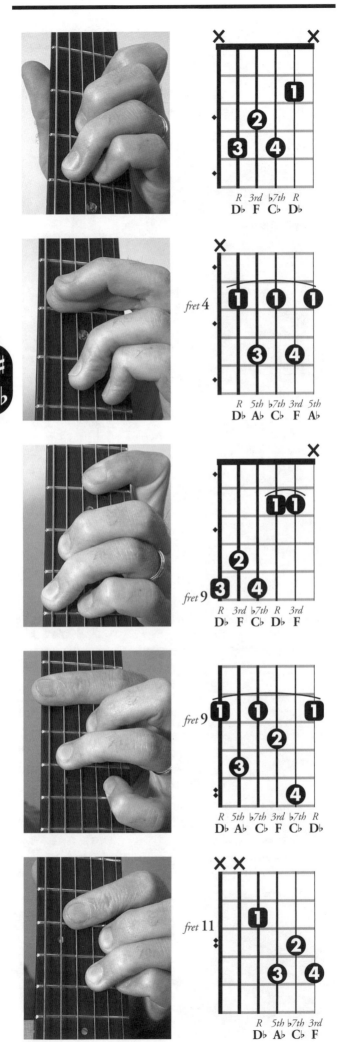

C♯
D♭

R   3rd   ♭7th R
D♭   F   C♭   D♭

fret 4
R   5th ♭7th 3rd 5th
D♭ A♭ C♭   F   A♭

fret 9
R   3rd ♭7th R   3rd
D♭ F   C♭   D♭ F

fret 9
R   5th ♭7th 3rd ♭7th R
D♭ A♭ C♭   F   C♭   D♭

fret 11
R   5th ♭7th 3rd
D♭ A♭ C♭   F

SCALE DEGREES: *R 3rd 5th ♭7th 9th*
CHORD TONES: **D♭ F A♭ C♭ E♭**

D♭9

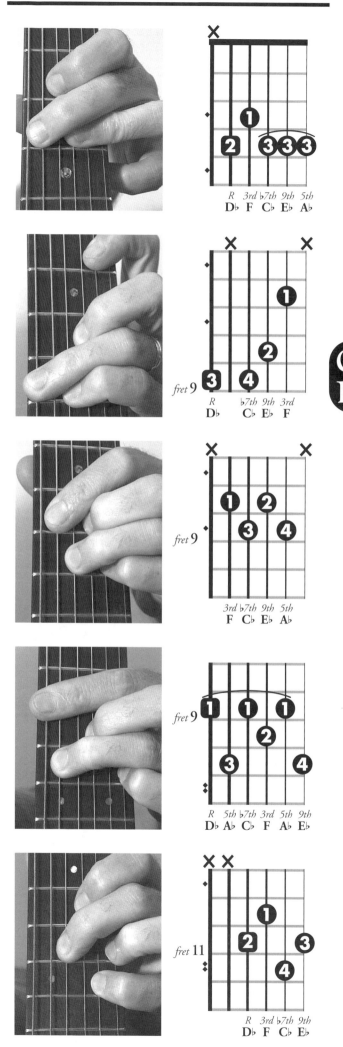

C#
D♭

Chord diagram labels:

1. R 3rd ♭7th 9th 5th / D♭ F C♭ E♭ A♭

2. fret 9 — R ♭7th 9th 3rd / D♭ C♭ E♭ F

3. fret 9 — 3rd ♭7th 9th 5th / F C♭ E♭ A♭

4. fret 9 — R 5th ♭7th 3rd 5th 9th / D♭ A♭ C♭ F A♭ E♭

5. fret 11 — R 3rd ♭7th 9th / D♭ F C♭ E♭

D♭7sus4

SCALE DEGREES: R 4th 5th ♭7th
CHORD TONES: D♭ G♭ A♭ C♭

C#
D♭

R 4th ♭7th R
D♭ G♭ C♭ D♭

fret 4

R 5th ♭7th 4th 5th
D♭ A♭ C♭ G♭ A♭

fret 6

5th R 4th ♭7th
A♭ D♭ G♭ C♭

fret 9

R 5th ♭7th 4th 5th R
D♭ A♭ C♭ G♭ A♭ D♭

fret 11

R 5th ♭7th 4th
D♭ A♭ C♭ G♭

SCALE DEGREES: *R 4th 5th ♭7th 9th*
CHORD TONES: D♭ G♭ A♭ C♭ E♭

D♭9sus4

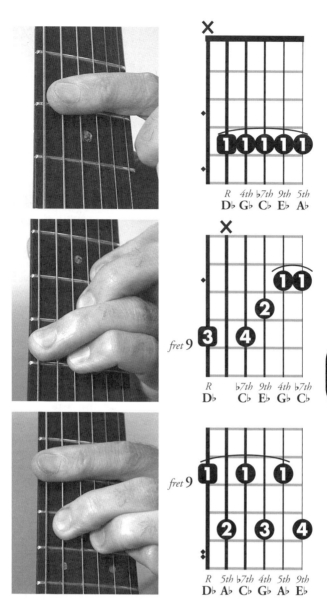

R   4th   ♭7th   9th   5th
D♭   G♭   C♭   E♭   A♭

fret 9

R   ♭7th   9th   4th   ♭7th
D♭   C♭   E♭   G♭   C♭

C#
D♭

fret 9

R   5th   ♭7th   4th   5th   9th
D♭   A♭   C♭   G♭   A♭   E♭

SCALE DEGREES: *R 3rd 5th ♭7th 9th 11th 13th*
CHORD TONES: D♭ F A♭ C♭ E♭ G♭ B♭

D♭13

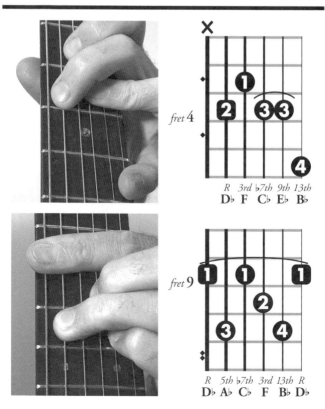

fret 4

R   3rd   ♭7th   9th   13th
D♭   F   C♭   E♭   B♭

fret 9

R   5th   ♭7th   3rd   13th   R
D♭   A♭   C♭   F   B♭   D♭

D♭7(♭5)

SCALE DEGREES: R 3rd ♭5th ♭7th
CHORD TONES: D♭ F A♭♭ C♭

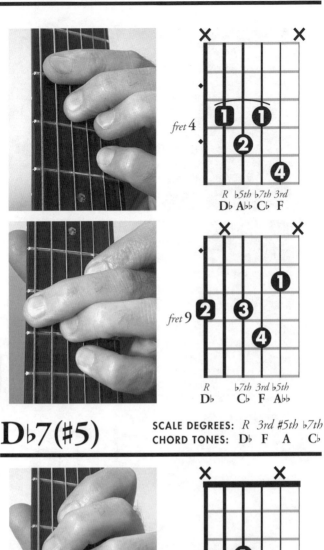

fret 4

R ♭5th ♭7th 3rd
D♭ A♭♭ C♭ F

fret 9

R ♭7th 3rd ♭5th
D♭ C♭ F A♭♭

D♭7(#5)

SCALE DEGREES: R 3rd #5th ♭7th
CHORD TONES: D♭ F A C♭

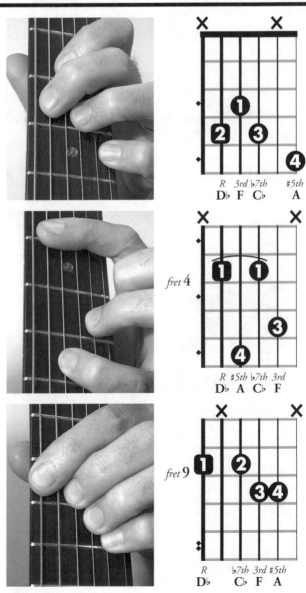

R 3rd ♭7th #5th
D♭ F C♭ A

fret 4

R #5th ♭7th 3rd
D♭ A C♭ F

fret 9

R ♭7th 3rd #5th
D♭ C♭ F A

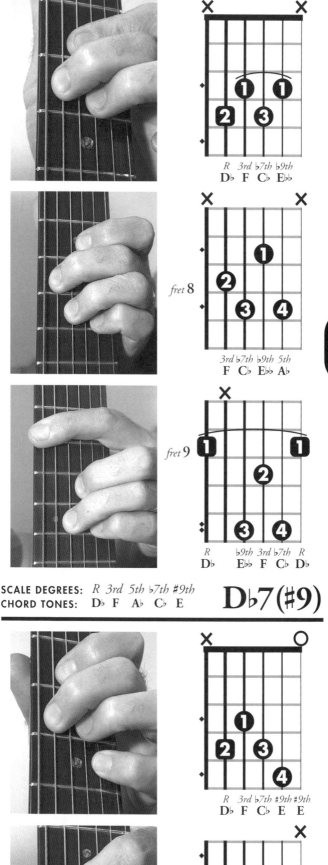

R   3rd ♭7th ♭9th
D♭   F   C♭   E♭♭

fret 8

3rd ♭7th ♭9th 5th
F   C♭   E♭♭   A♭

fret 9

R   ♭9th 3rd ♭7th   R
D♭   E♭♭   F   C♭   D♭

SCALE DEGREES: *R* *3rd* *5th* *♭7th* *#9th*
CHORD TONES: **D♭** **F** **A♭** **C♭** **E**

D♭7(#9)

R   3rd ♭7th #9th #9th
D♭   F   C♭   E   E

fret 9

R   3rd ♭7th #9th 5th
D♭   F   C♭   E   A♭

D♭9(♭5)

SCALE DEGREES: R 3rd ♭5th ♭7th 9th
CHORD TONES: D♭ F A♭♭ C♭ E♭

R 3rd ♭7th 9th ♭5th
D♭ F C♭ E♭ A♭♭

R 3rd ♭7th 9th ♭5th
D♭ F C♭ E♭ A♭♭

fret 9

D♭9(#5)

SCALE DEGREES: R 3rd #5th ♭7th 9th
CHORD TONES: D♭ F A C♭ E♭

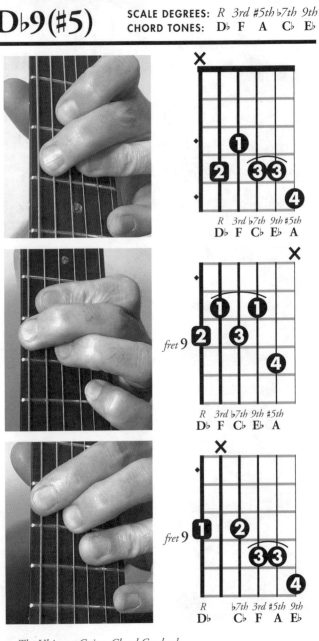

R 3rd ♭7th 9th #5th
D♭ F C♭ E♭ A

R 3rd ♭7th 9th #5th
D♭ F C♭ E♭ A

fret 9

R ♭7th 3rd #5th 9th
D♭ C♭ F A E♭

fret 9

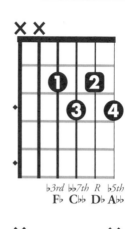

♭3rd ♭♭7th R ♭5th
F♭ C♭♭ D♭ A♭♭

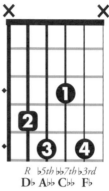

R ♭5th ♭♭7th ♭3rd
D♭ A♭♭ C♭♭ F♭

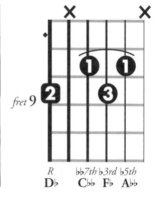

fret 9

R ♭♭7th ♭3rd ♭5th
D♭ C♭♭ F♭ A♭♭

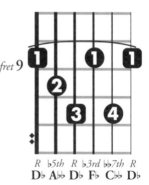

fret 9

R ♭5th R ♭3rd ♭♭7th R
D♭ A♭♭ D♭ F♭ C♭♭ D♭

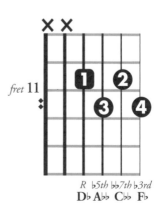

fret 11

R ♭5th ♭♭7th ♭3rd
D♭ A♭♭ C♭♭ F♭

C♯
D♭

D

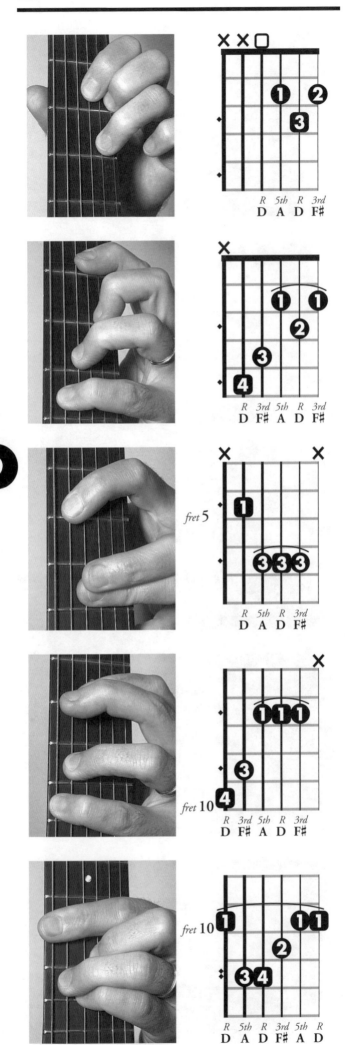

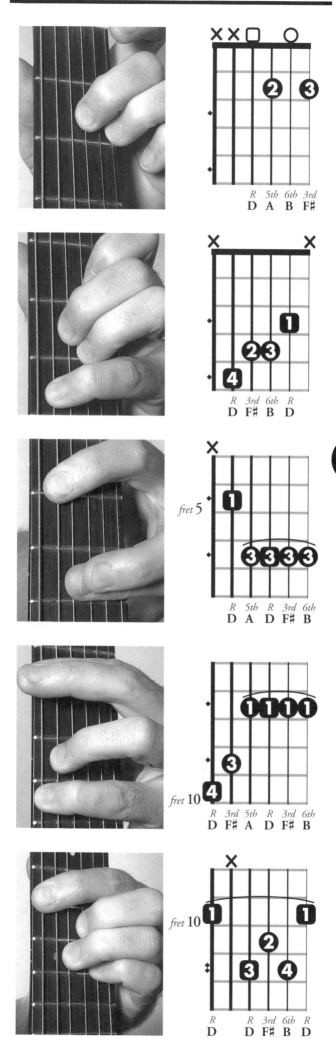

Dmaj7

R 5th 7th 3rd
D A C# F#

R 3rd 5th 7th 3rd
D F# A C# F#

fret 5

R 5th 7th 3rd 5th
D A C# F# A

fret 10

R   7th 3rd 5th
D   C# F# A

fret 12

R 3rd 5th 7th
D F# A C#

SCALE DEGREES: *R   3rd 5th 9th*
CHORD TONES: D   F#   A   E

D(9)

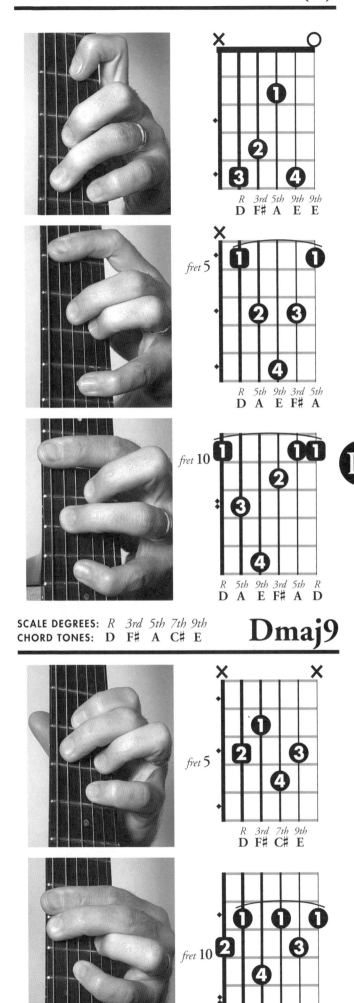

R	3rd	5th	9th	9th
D	F#	A	E	E

fret 5

R	5th	9th	3rd	5th
D	A	E	F#	A

fret 10

D

R	5th	9th	3rd	5th	R
D	A	E	F#	A	D

SCALE DEGREES: *R   3rd 5th 7th 9th*
CHORD TONES: D   F#   A   C#   E

Dmaj9

fret 5

R	3rd	7th	9th
D	F#	C#	E

fret 10

R	3rd	7th	9th	5th	7th
D	F#	C#	E	A	C#

Dmaj7(♯11)
SCALE DEGREES: *R 3rd 5th 7th ♯11th*
CHORD TONES: D F♯ A C♯ G♯

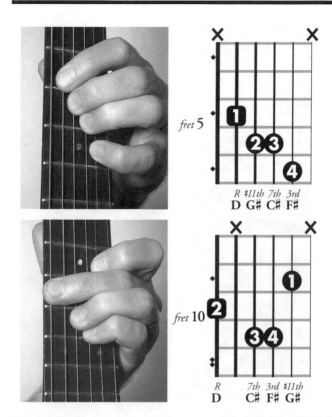

fret 5

R   ♯11th   7th   3rd
D   G♯   C♯   F♯

fret 10

R   7th   3rd   ♯11th
D   C♯   F♯   G♯

D6/9
SCALE DEGREES: *R 3rd 5th 6th 9th*
CHORD TONES: D F♯ A B E

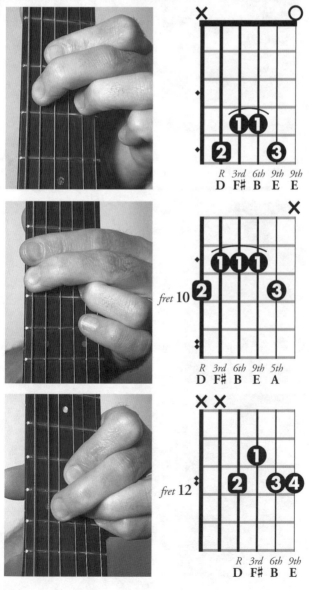

R   3rd   6th   9th   9th
D   F♯   B   E   E

fret 10

R   3rd   6th   9th   5th
D   F♯   B   E   A

fret 12

R   3rd   6th   9th
D   F♯   B   E

Dsus2

×	×	□			○
			①		
				③	

R 5th R 2nd
D A D E

×

fret 5

| | ① | | ① | ① |
| | | ③ | ④ | |

R 5th R 2nd 5th
D A D E A

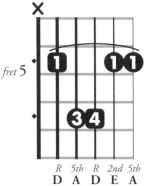

Dsus4

D

×	×	□			
			①		
				③	④

R 5th R 4th
D A D G

fret 5

①	①			①
		③		
			④	

R 4th R 4th 5th
D G D G A

fret 10

| ① | ① | | | ① | ① |
| | | ③ | ④ | | |

R 4th R 4th 5th R
D G D G A D

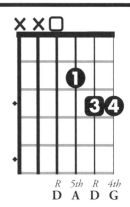

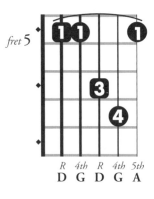

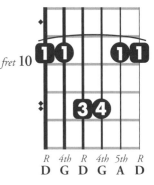

The Ultimate Guitar Chord Casebook   119

Dm

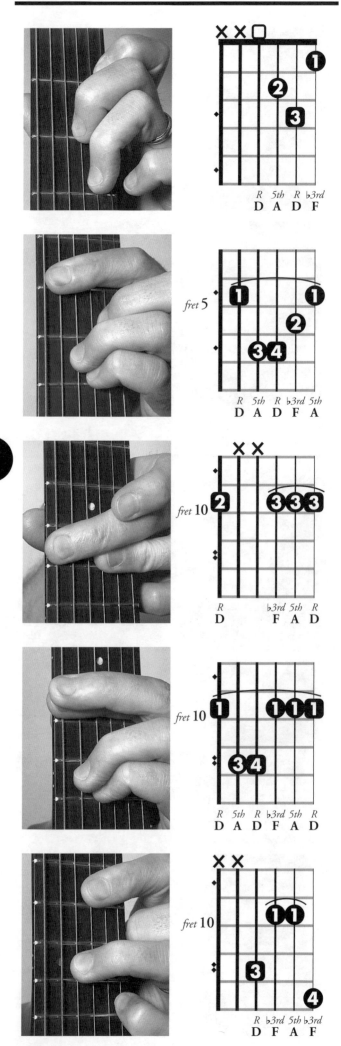

Dm6

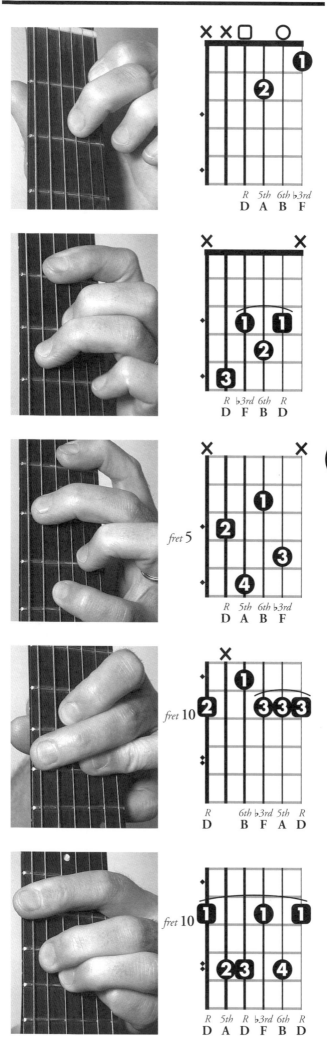

Dm7

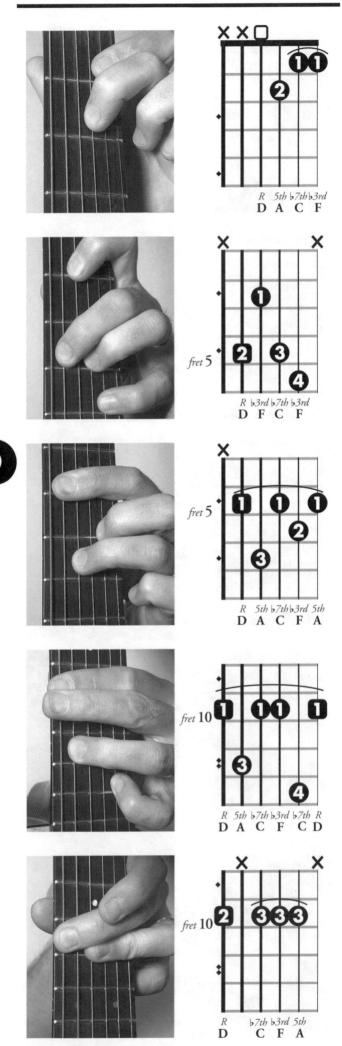

R 5th ♭7th ♭3rd
D A C F

fret 5

R ♭3rd ♭7th ♭3rd
D F C F

fret 5

R 5th ♭7th ♭3rd 5th
D A C F A

fret 10

R 5th ♭7th ♭3rd ♭7th R
D A C F C D

fret 10

R ♭7th ♭3rd 5th
D C F A

D

SCALE DEGREES: R ♭3rd ♭5th ♭7th
CHORD TONES: D F A♭ C

Dm7(♭5)

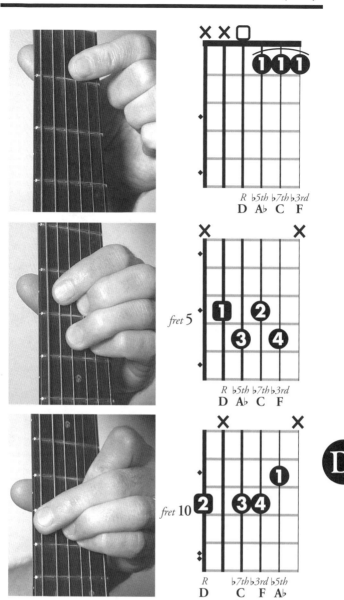

R ♭5th ♭7th ♭3rd
D A♭ C F

fret 5

R ♭5th ♭7th ♭3rd
D A♭ C F

fret 10

R   ♭7th ♭3rd ♭5th
D   C F A♭

D

SCALE DEGREES: R ♭3rd 5th ♭7th 9th
CHORD TONES: D F A C E

Dm9

R ♭3rd ♭7th 9th 9th
D F C E E

fret 10

R 5th ♭7th ♭3rd 5th 9th
D A C F A E

Dm(maj7)

SCALE DEGREES: *R ♭3rd 5th 7th*
CHORD TONES: D F A C#

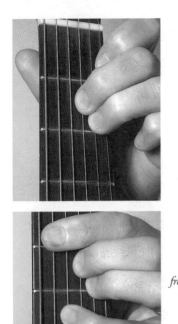

X X ▢

①
② ③

R 5th 7th ♭3rd
D A C# F

fret 5

①   ①
② ③
④

R 5th 7th ♭3rd 5th
D A C# F A

Dm(9)

SCALE DEGREES: *R ♭3rd 5th 9th*
CHORD TONES: D F A E

D

X   ○

①
②
③   ④

R ♭3rd 5th 9th 9th
D F A E E

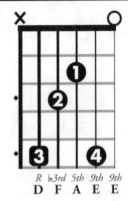

fret 5

①   ①
②
③
④

R 5th 9th ♭3rd 5th
D A E F A

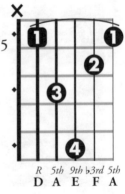

fret 10

①   ① ①
② ③   ④

R 5th R ♭3rd 5th 9th
D A D F A E

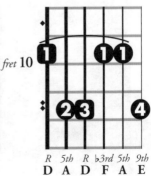

SCALE DEGREES: *R ♭3rd 5th ♭7th 9th 11th*
CHORD TONES: D F A C E G

Dm11

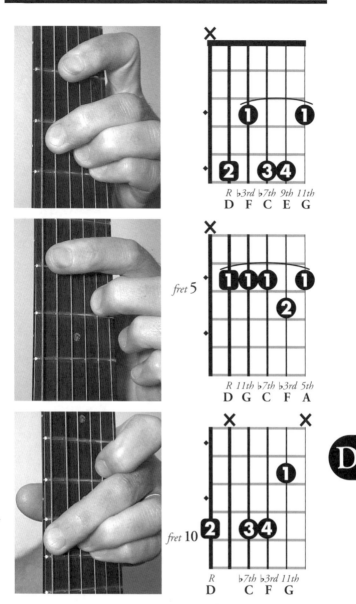

R ♭3rd ♭7th 9th 11th
D F C E G

fret 5

R 11th ♭7th ♭3rd 5th
D G C F A

fret 10

R   ♭7th ♭3rd 11th
D   C F G

SCALE DEGREES: *R ♭3rd 5th ♭7th 9th 11th 13th*
CHORD TONES: D F A C E G B

Dm13

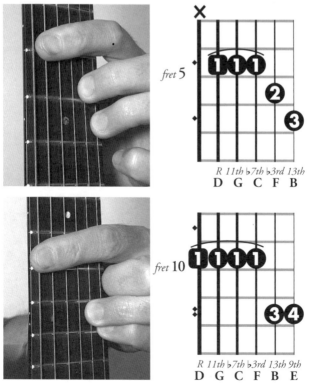

fret 5

R 11th ♭7th ♭3rd 13th
D G C F B

fret 10

R 11th ♭7th ♭3rd 13th 9th
D G C F B E

D7

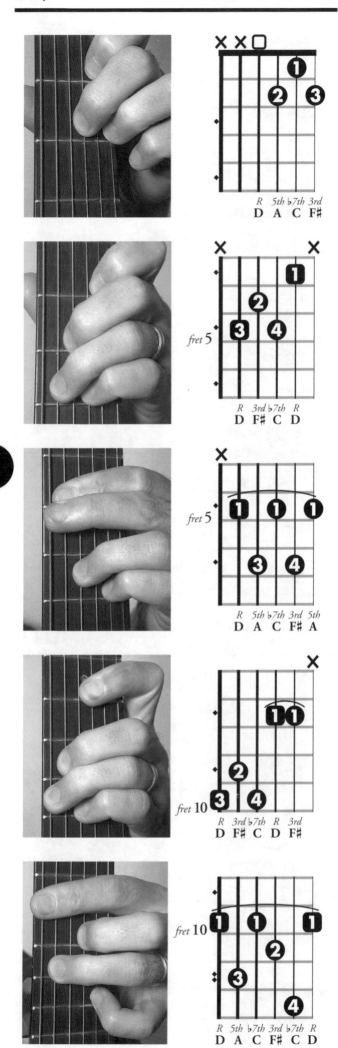

R 5th ♭7th 3rd
D A C F#

R 3rd ♭7th R
D F# C D

R 5th ♭7th 3rd 5th
D A C F# A

R 3rd ♭7th R 3rd
D F# C D F#

R 5th ♭7th 3rd ♭7th R
D A C F# C D

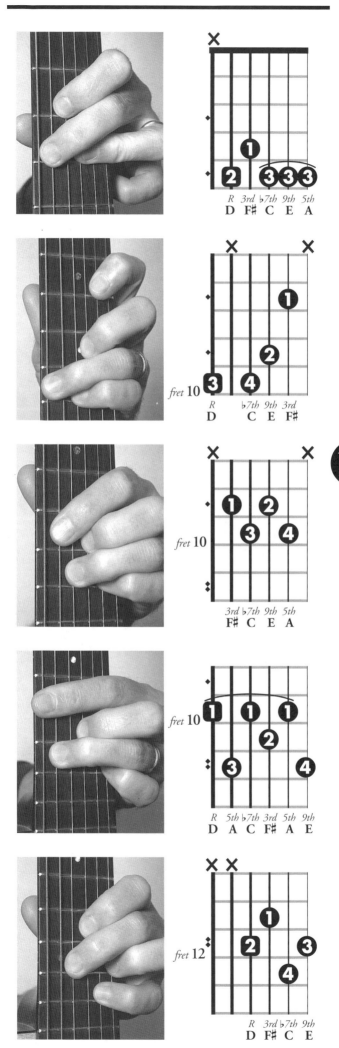

R   3rd   ♭7th   9th   5th
D   F#   C   E   A

fret 10
R   ♭7th   9th   3rd
D   C   E   F#

D

fret 10
3rd   ♭7th   9th   5th
F#   C   E   A

fret 10
R   5th   ♭7th   3rd   5th   9th
D   A   C   F#   A   E

fret 12
R   3rd   ♭7th   9th
D   F#   C   E

D7sus4

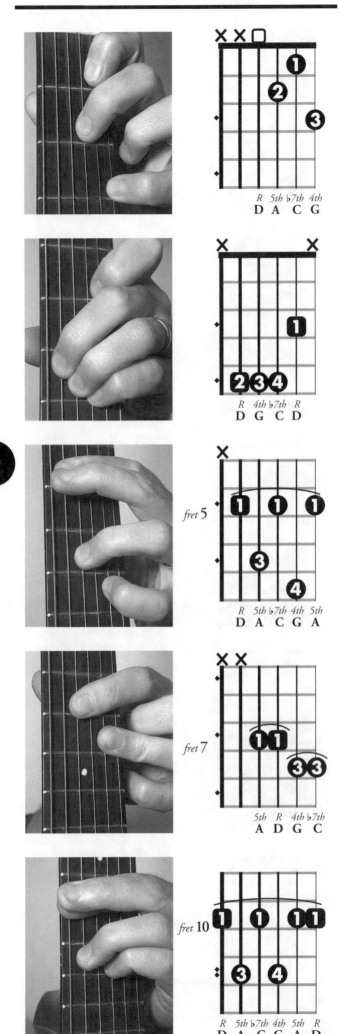

D

fret 5

fret 7

fret 10

R 5th ♭7th 4th
D A C G

R 4th ♭7th R
D G C D

R 5th ♭7th 4th 5th
D A C G A

5th R 4th ♭7th
A D G C

R 5th ♭7th 4th 5th R
D A C G A D

SCALE DEGREES: *R 4th 5th ♭7th 9th*
CHORD TONES: D G A C E

D9sus4

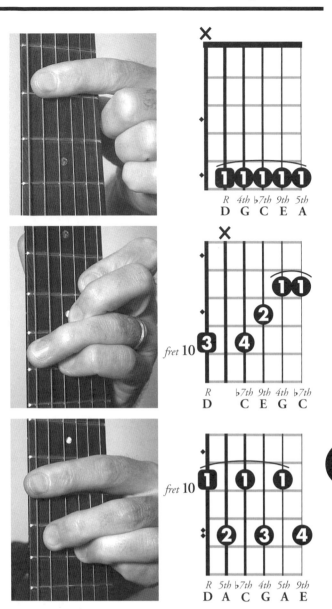

SCALE DEGREES: *R 3rd 5th ♭7th 9th 11th 13th*
CHORD TONES: D F♯ A C E G B

D13

D

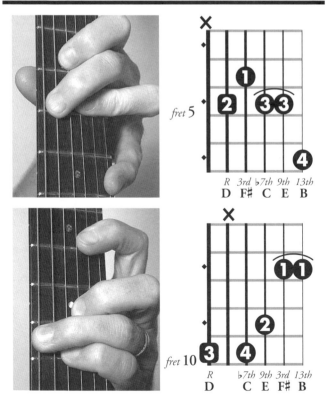

D7(♭5)

SCALE DEGREES: R 3rd ♭5th ♭7th
CHORD TONES: D F# A♭ C

× × ○

R ♭5th ♭7th 3rd
D A♭ C F#

×   ×

fret 5

R ♭5th ♭7th 3rd
D A♭ C F#

D7(#5)

SCALE DEGREES: R 3rd #5th ♭7th
CHORD TONES: D F# A# C

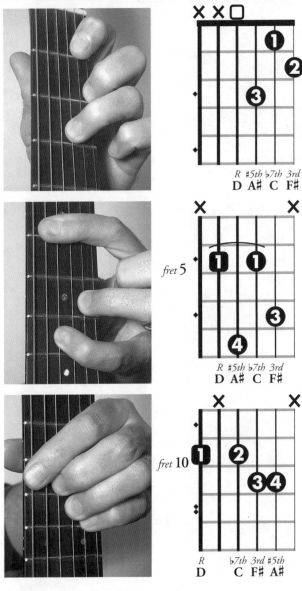

× × ○

R #5th ♭7th 3rd
D A# C F#

×   ×

fret 5

R #5th ♭7th 3rd
D A# C F#

×   ×

fret 10

R   ♭7th 3rd #5th
D   C F# A#

SCALE DEGREES: R 3rd 5th ♭7th ♭9th
CHORD TONES: D F♯ A C E♭

D7(♭9)

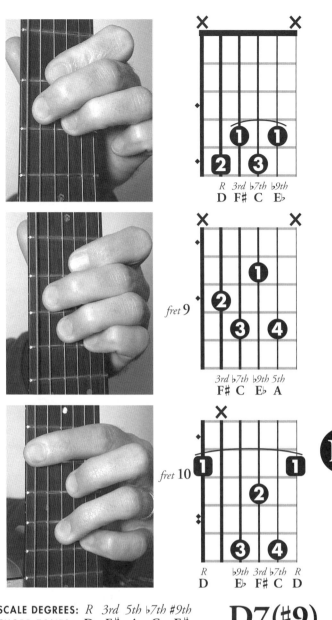

R 3rd ♭7th ♭9th
D F♯ C E♭

fret 9

3rd ♭7th ♭9th 5th
F♯ C E♭ A

fret 10

R ♭9th 3rd ♭7th R
D E♭ F♯ C D

D

SCALE DEGREES: R 3rd 5th ♭7th ♯9th
CHORD TONES: D F♯ A C E♯

D7(♯9)

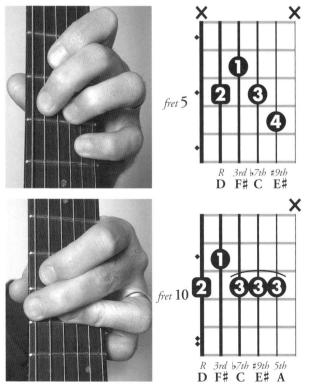

fret 5

R 3rd ♭7th ♯9th
D F♯ C E♯

fret 10

R 3rd ♭7th ♯9th 5th
D F♯ C E♯ A

D9(♭5)

SCALE DEGREES: R 3rd ♭5th ♭7th 9th
CHORD TONES: D F# A♭ C E

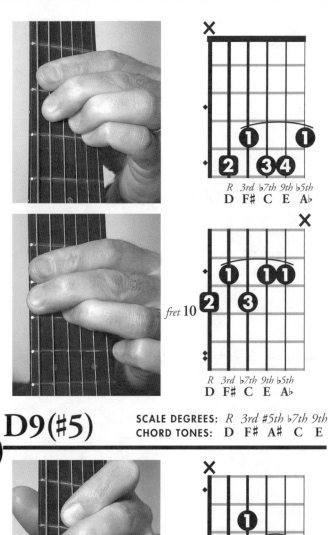

R 3rd ♭7th 9th ♭5th
D F# C   E   A♭

R 3rd ♭7th 9th ♭5th
D F# C   E   A♭ (fret 10)

D9(#5)

SCALE DEGREES: R 3rd #5th ♭7th 9th
CHORD TONES: D F# A# C E

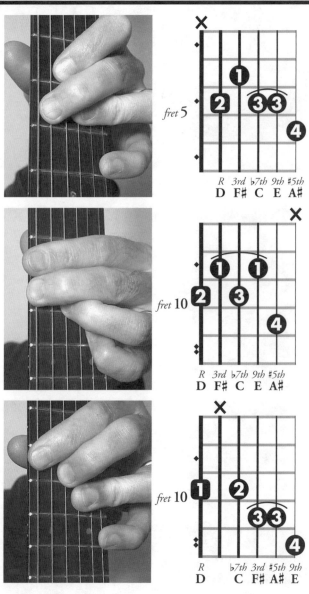

R 3rd ♭7th 9th #5th
D F# C   E   A# (fret 5)

R 3rd ♭7th 9th #5th
D F# C   E   A# (fret 10)

R   ♭7th 3rd #5th 9th
D   C   F#   A#   E (fret 10)

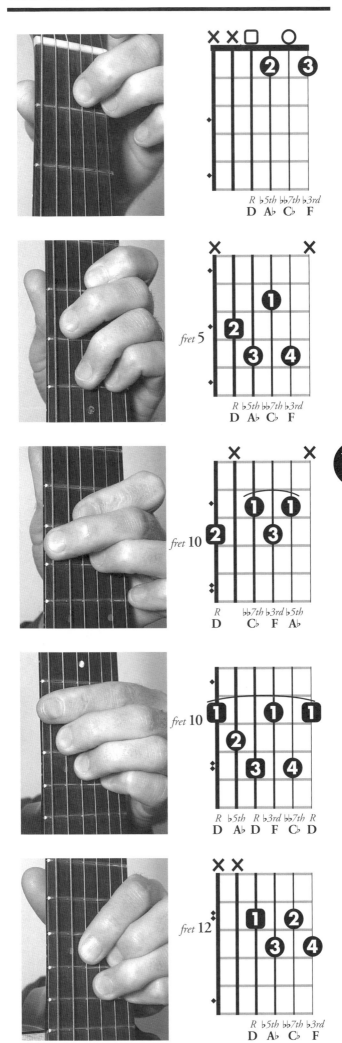

R ♭5th ♭♭7th ♭3rd
D A♭ C♭ F

fret 5

R ♭5th ♭♭7th ♭3rd
D A♭ C♭ F

D

fret 10

R ♭♭7th ♭3rd ♭5th
D C♭ F A♭

fret 10

R ♭5th R ♭3rd ♭♭7th R
D A♭ D F C♭ D

fret 12

R ♭5th ♭♭7th ♭3rd
D A♭ C♭ F

E♭

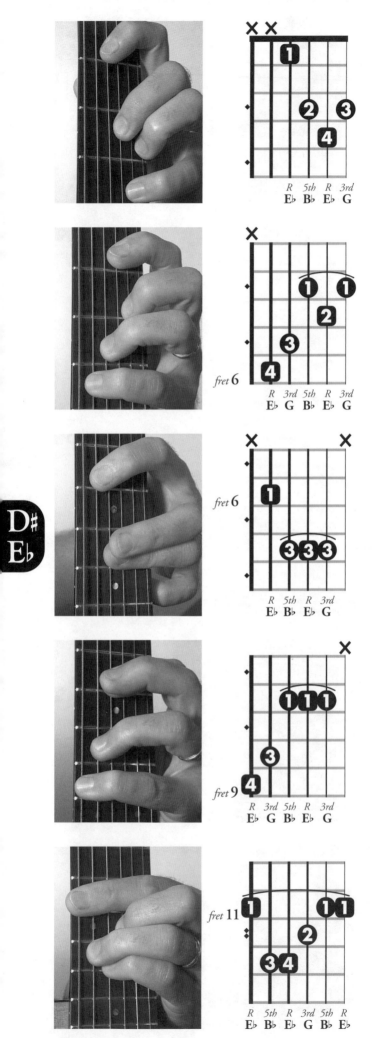

fret 6

fret 6

fret 9

fret 11

R   5th   R   3rd
E♭   B♭   E♭   G

R   3rd   5th   R   3rd
E♭   G   B♭   E♭   G

R   5th   R   3rd
E♭   B♭   E♭   G

R   3rd   5th   R   3rd
E♭   G   B♭   E♭   G

R   5th   R   3rd   5th   R
E♭   B♭   E♭   G   B♭   E♭

D#
E♭

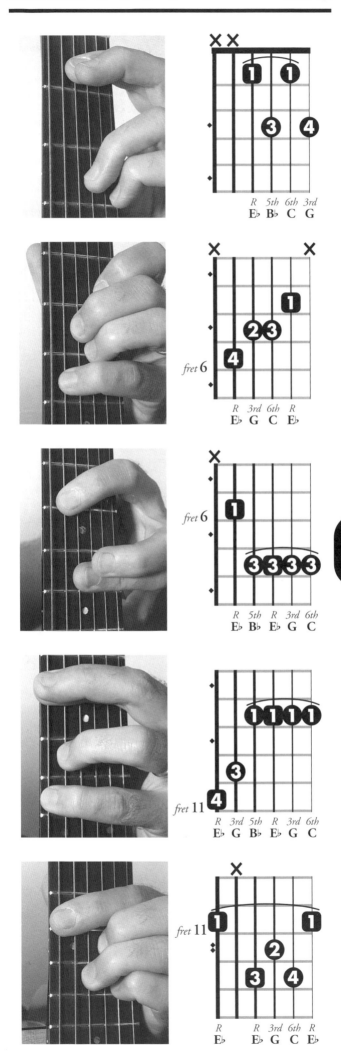

D#
E♭

E♭maj7

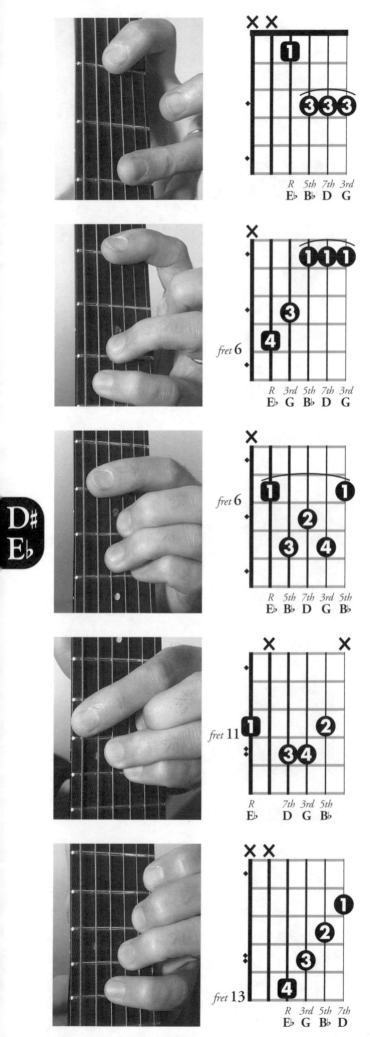

SCALE DEGREES: *R 3rd 5th 9th*
CHORD TONES: Eb G Bb F

Eb(9)

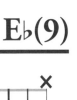
fret 6

R 3rd 5th 9th
Eb G Bb F

fret 6

R 5th 9th 3rd 5th
Eb Bb F G Bb

fret 11

R 5th 9th 3rd 5th R
Eb Bb F G Bb Eb

SCALE DEGREES: *R 3rd 5th 7th 9th*
CHORD TONES: Eb G Bb D F

Ebmaj9

fret 6

R 3rd 7th 9th
Eb G D F

fret 11

R 3rd 7th 9th 5th 7th
Eb G D F Bb D

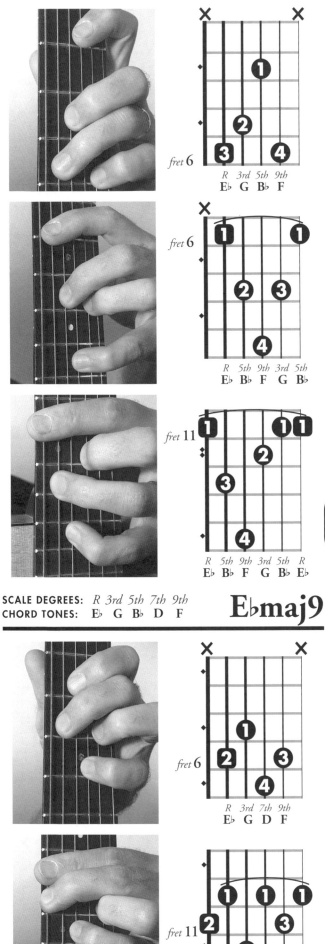

E♭maj7(♯11)
SCALE DEGREES: *R 3rd 5th 7th ♯11th*
CHORD TONES: E♭ G B♭ D A

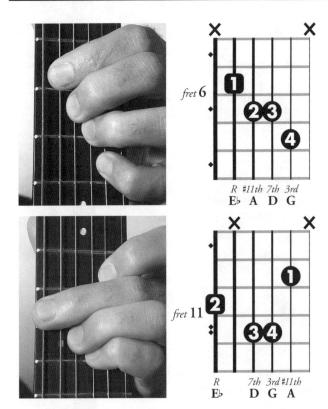

R	♯11th	7th	3rd
E♭	A	D	G

fret 6

R		7th	3rd ♯11th
E♭		D	G A

fret 11

E♭6/9
SCALE DEGREES: *R 3rd 5th 6th 9th*
CHORD TONES: E♭ G B♭ C F

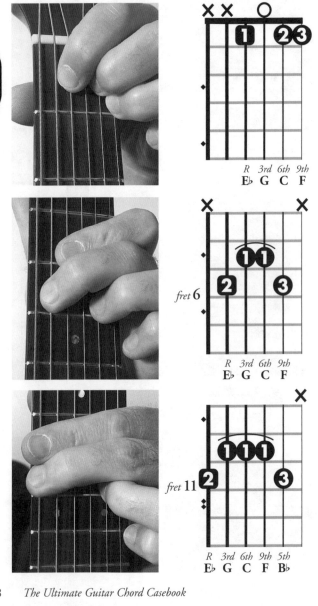

R	3rd	6th	9th
E♭	G	C	F

fret 6

R	3rd	6th	9th
E♭	G	C	F

fret 11

R	3rd	6th	9th	5th
E♭	G	C	F	B♭

D♯
E♭

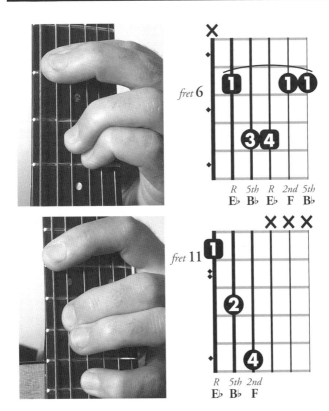

fret 6

R	5th	R	2nd	5th
E♭	B♭	E♭	F	B♭

fret 11

R	5th	2nd
E♭	B♭	F

SCALE DEGREES: *R 4th 5th*
CHORD TONES: **E♭ A♭ B♭**

E♭sus4

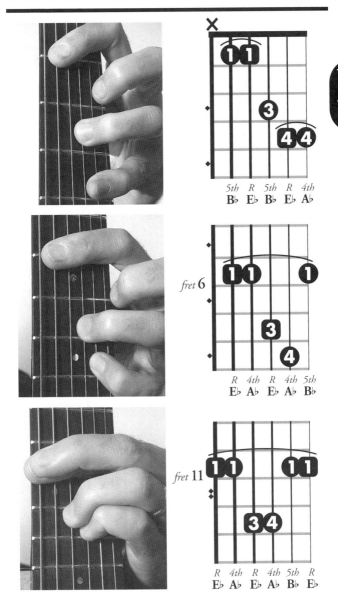

5th	R	5th	R	4th
B♭	E♭	B♭	E♭	A♭

fret 6

R	4th	R	4th	5th
E♭	A♭	E♭	A♭	B♭

fret 11

R	4th	R	4th	5th	R
E♭	A♭	E♭	A♭	B♭	E♭

D#
E♭

E♭m

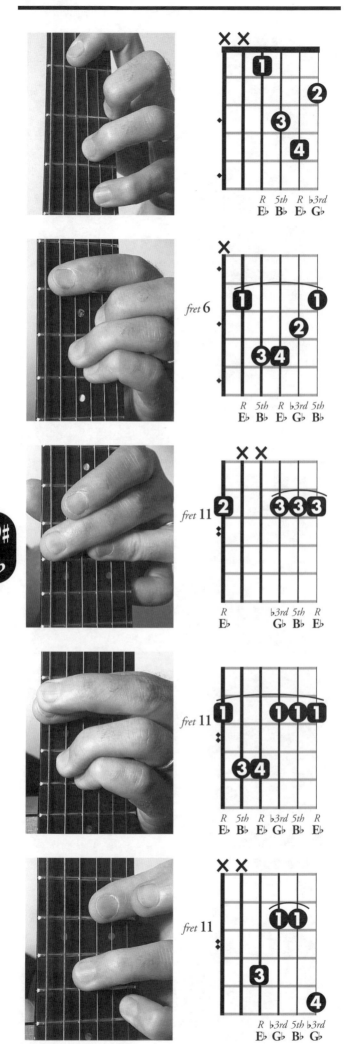

× ×
1
2
3
4

R 5th R ♭3rd
E♭ B♭ E♭ G♭

×
fret 6
1 1
2
3 4

R 5th R ♭3rd 5th
E♭ B♭ E♭ G♭ B♭

× ×
fret 11
2 3 3 3

R ♭3rd 5th R
E♭ G♭ B♭ E♭

fret 11
1 1 1 1
3 4

R 5th R ♭3rd 5th R
E♭ B♭ E♭ G♭ B♭ E♭

× ×
fret 11
1 1
3
4

R ♭3rd 5th ♭3rd
E♭ G♭ B♭ G♭

D#
E♭

E♭m6

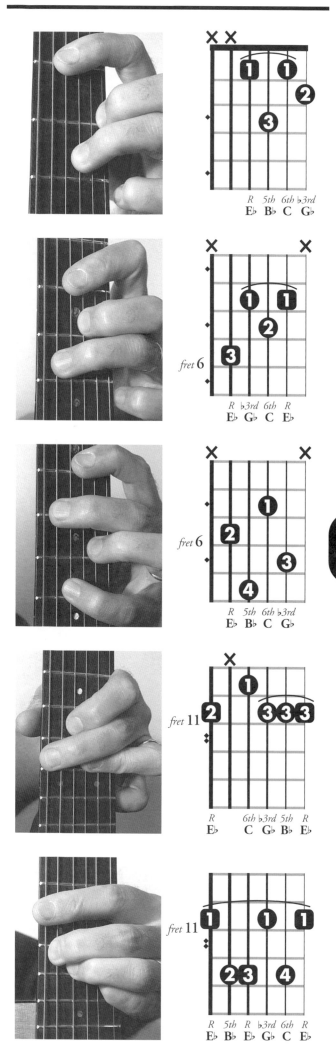

R   5th 6th ♭3rd
E♭ B♭   C   G♭

fret 6

R   ♭3rd 6th R
E♭ G♭   C   E♭

fret 6

R   5th 6th ♭3rd
E♭ B♭   C   G♭

D#
E♭

fret 11

R   6th ♭3rd 5th R
E♭   C   G♭   B♭   E♭

fret 11

R   5th R ♭3rd 6th R
E♭ B♭   E♭ G♭   C   E♭

E♭m7

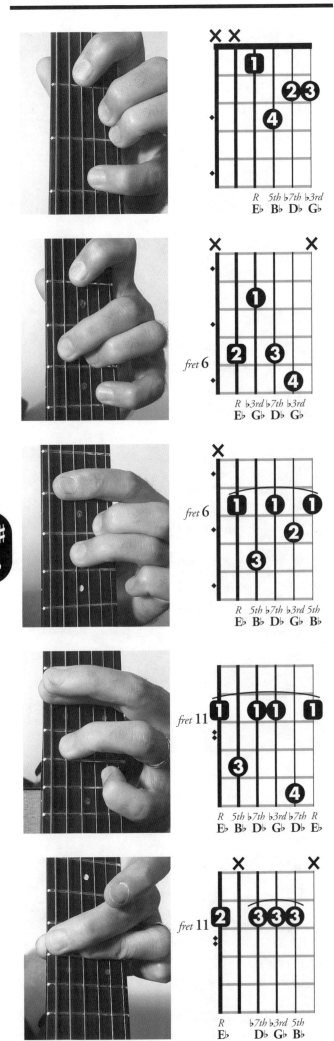

R 5th ♭7th ♭3rd
E♭ B♭ D♭ G♭

fret 6

R ♭3rd ♭7th ♭3rd
E♭ G♭ D♭ G♭

fret 6

R 5th ♭7th ♭3rd 5th
E♭ B♭ D♭ G♭ B♭

fret 11

R 5th ♭7th ♭3rd ♭7th R
E♭ B♭ D♭ G♭ D♭ E♭

fret 11

R ♭7th ♭3rd 5th
E♭ D♭ G♭ B♭

D#
E♭

E♭m7(♭5)

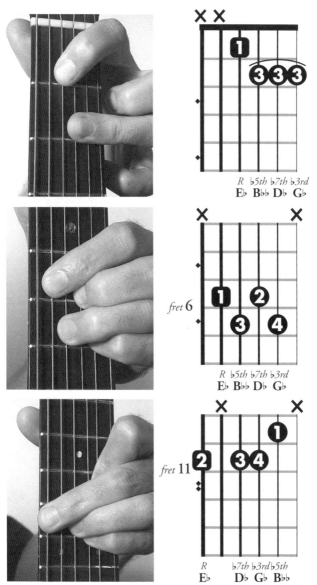

R ♭5th ♭7th ♭3rd
E♭ B♭♭ D♭ G♭

fret 6

R ♭5th ♭7th ♭3rd
E♭ B♭♭ D♭ G♭

fret 11

R ♭7th ♭3rd ♭5th
E♭ D♭ G♭ B♭♭

**D♯
E♭**

E♭m9

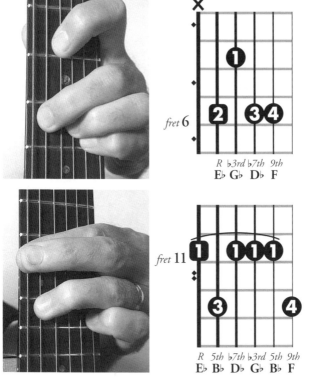

fret 6

R ♭3rd ♭7th 9th
E♭ G♭ D♭ F

fret 11

R 5th ♭7th ♭3rd 5th 9th
E♭ B♭ D♭ G♭ B♭ F

E♭m(maj7)

SCALE DEGREES: R ♭3rd 5th 7th
CHORD TONES: E♭ G♭ B♭ D

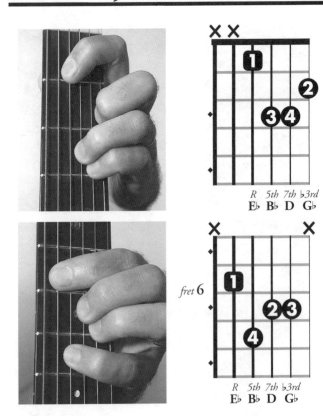

R 5th 7th ♭3rd
E♭ B♭ D G♭

fret 6

R 5th 7th ♭3rd
E♭ B♭ D G♭

E♭m(9)

SCALE DEGREES: R ♭3rd 5th 9th
CHORD TONES: E♭ G♭ B♭ F

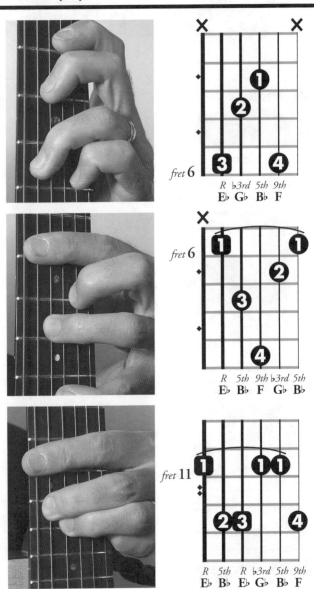

fret 6

R ♭3rd 5th 9th
E♭ G♭ B♭ F

fret 6

R 5th 9th ♭3rd 5th
E♭ B♭ F G♭ B♭

fret 11

R 5th R ♭3rd 5th 9th
E♭ B♭ E♭ G♭ B♭ F

D#
E♭

SCALE DEGREES: *R ♭3rd 5th ♭7th 9th 11th*
CHORD TONES: **E♭ G♭ B♭ D♭ F A♭**

E♭m11

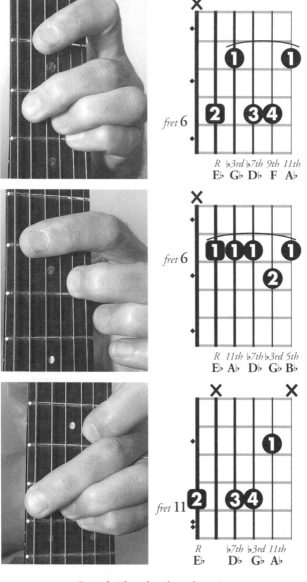

R ♭3rd ♭7th 9th 11th
E♭ G♭ D♭ F A♭

R 11th ♭7th ♭3rd 5th
E♭ A♭ D♭ G♭ B♭

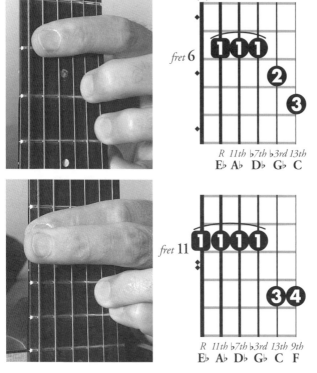

R ♭7th ♭3rd 11th
E♭ D♭ G♭ A♭

D#
E♭

SCALE DEGREES: *R ♭3rd 5th ♭7th 9th 11th 13th*
CHORD TONES: **E♭ G♭ B♭ D♭ F A♭ C**

E♭m13

R 11th ♭7th ♭3rd 13th
E♭ A♭ D♭ G♭ C

R 11th ♭7th ♭3rd 13th 9th
E♭ A♭ D♭ G♭ C F

E♭7

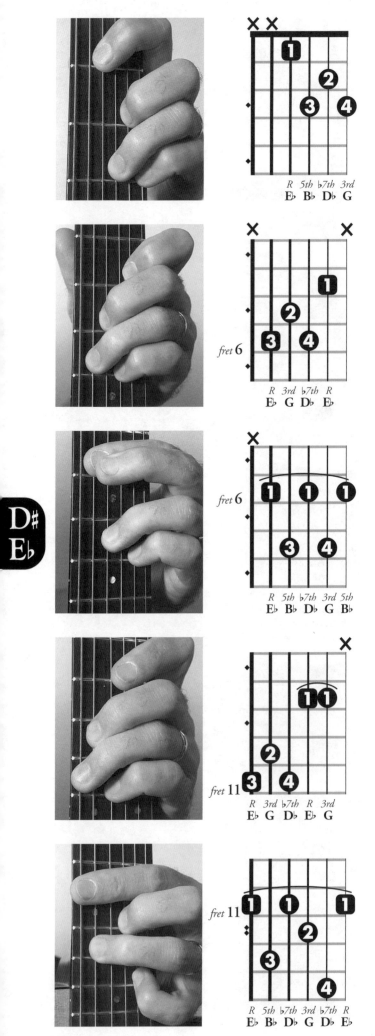

R   5th ♭7th 3rd
E♭ B♭ D♭   G

fret 6

R   3rd ♭7th R
E♭ G   D♭   E♭

fret 6

R   5th ♭7th 3rd 5th
E♭ B♭ D♭   G   B♭

fret 11

R   3rd ♭7th R   3rd
E♭ G   D♭   E♭ G

fret 11

R   5th ♭7th 3rd ♭7th R
E♭ B♭ D♭   G   D♭   E♭

D#
E♭

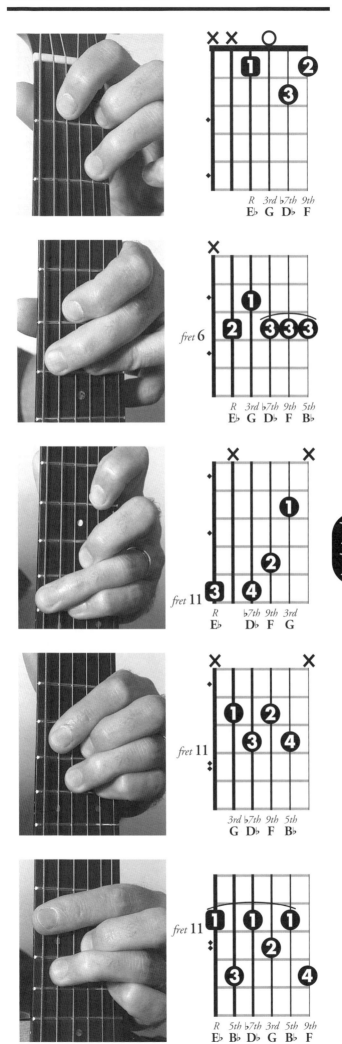

fret 6

fret 11

fret 11

fret 11

D#
E♭

		R	*3rd*	*♭7th*	*9th*
		E♭	G	D♭	F

	R	*3rd*	*♭7th*	*9th*	*5th*
	E♭	G	D♭	F	B♭

	R		*♭7th*	*9th*	*3rd*
	E♭		D♭	F	G

		3rd	*♭7th*	*9th*	*5th*
		G	D♭	F	B♭

R	*5th*	*♭7th*	*3rd*	*5th*	*9th*
E♭	B♭	D♭	G	B♭	F

E♭7sus4

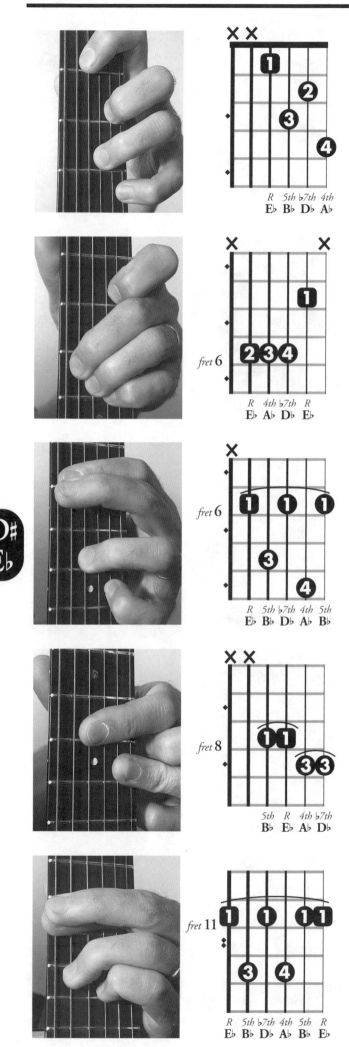

R 5th ♭7th 4th
E♭ B♭ D♭ A♭

fret 6

R 4th ♭7th R
E♭ A♭ D♭ E♭

fret 6

R 5th ♭7th 4th 5th
E♭ B♭ D♭ A♭ B♭

D#
E♭

fret 8

5th R 4th ♭7th
B♭ E♭ A♭ D♭

fret 11

R 5th ♭7th 4th 5th R
E♭ B♭ D♭ A♭ B♭ E♭

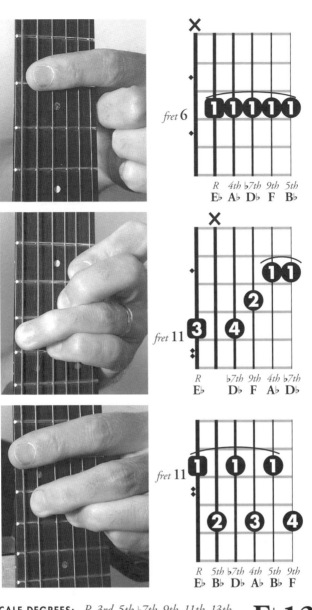

fret 6

R	4th	♭7th	9th	5th
E♭	A♭	D♭	F	B♭

fret 11

R		♭7th	9th	4th	♭7th
E♭		D♭	F	A♭	D♭

fret 11

R	5th	♭7th	4th	5th	9th
E♭	B♭	D♭	A♭	B♭	F

D#
E♭

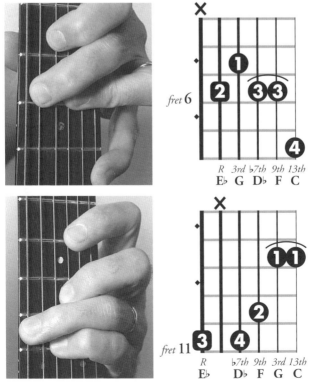

fret 6

R	3rd	♭7th	9th	13th
E♭	G	D♭	F	C

fret 11

R		♭7th	9th	3rd	13th
E♭		D♭	F	G	C

E♭7(♭5)

SCALE DEGREES:	R	3rd	♭5th	♭7th
CHORD TONES:	E♭	G	B♭♭	D♭

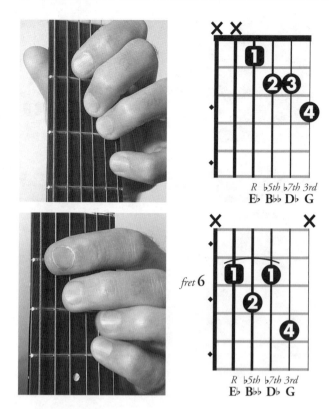

R ♭5th ♭7th 3rd
E♭ B♭♭ D♭ G

fret 6

R ♭5th ♭7th 3rd
E♭ B♭♭ D♭ G

E♭7(♯5)

SCALE DEGREES:	R	3rd	♯5th	♭7th
CHORD TONES:	E♭	G	B	D♭

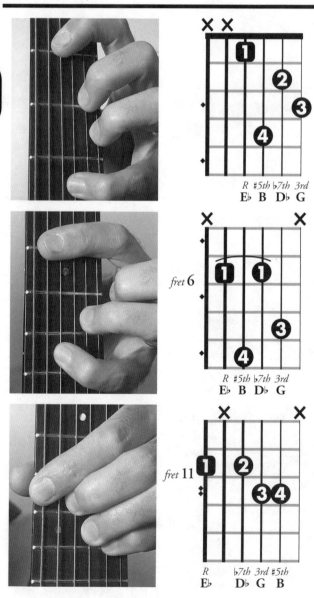

R ♯5th ♭7th 3rd
E♭ B D♭ G

fret 6

R ♯5th ♭7th 3rd
E♭ B D♭ G

fret 11

R ♭7th 3rd ♯5th
E♭ D♭ G B

D♯
E♭

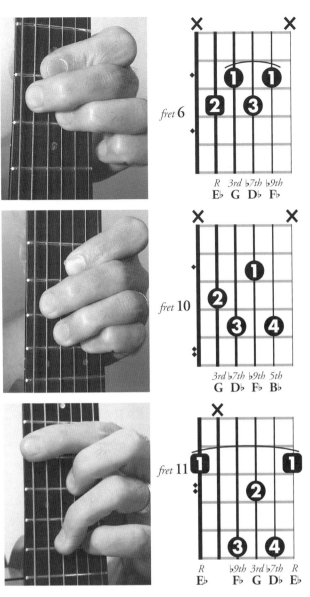

R 3rd ♭7th ♭9th
E♭ G D♭ F♭

3rd ♭7th ♭9th 5th
G D♭ F♭ B♭

R ♭9th 3rd ♭7th R
E♭ F♭ G D♭ E♭

D#
E♭

SCALE DEGREES: *R 3rd 5th ♭7th #9th*	**E♭7(#9)**
CHORD TONES: E♭ G B♭ D♭ F#	

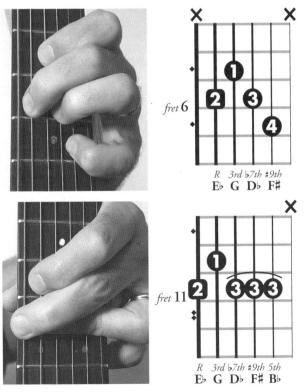

R 3rd ♭7th #9th
E♭ G D♭ F#

R 3rd ♭7th #9th 5th
E♭ G D♭ F# B♭

The Ultimate Guitar Chord Casebook   151

E♭9(♭5)

SCALE DEGREES: R   3rd   ♭5th   ♭7th   9th
CHORD TONES: E♭   G   B♭♭   D♭   F

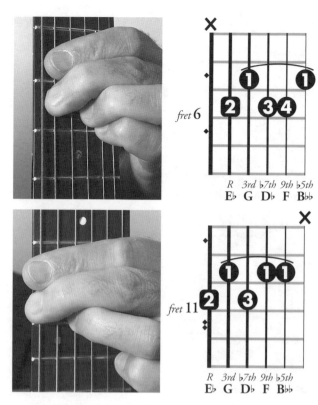

fret 6

R   3rd   ♭7th   9th   ♭5th
E♭   G   D♭   F   B♭♭

fret 11

R   3rd   ♭7th   9th   ♭5th
E♭   G   D♭   F   B♭♭

E♭9(#5)

SCALE DEGREES: R   3rd   #5th   ♭7th   9th
CHORD TONES: E♭   G   B   D♭   F

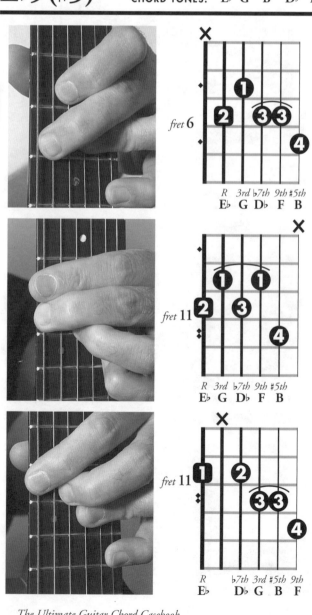

fret 6

R   3rd   ♭7th   9th   #5th
E♭   G   D♭   F   B

fret 11

R   3rd   ♭7th   9th   #5th
E♭   G   D♭   F   B

fret 11

R   ♭7th   3rd   #5th   9th
E♭   D♭   G   B   F

D#
E♭

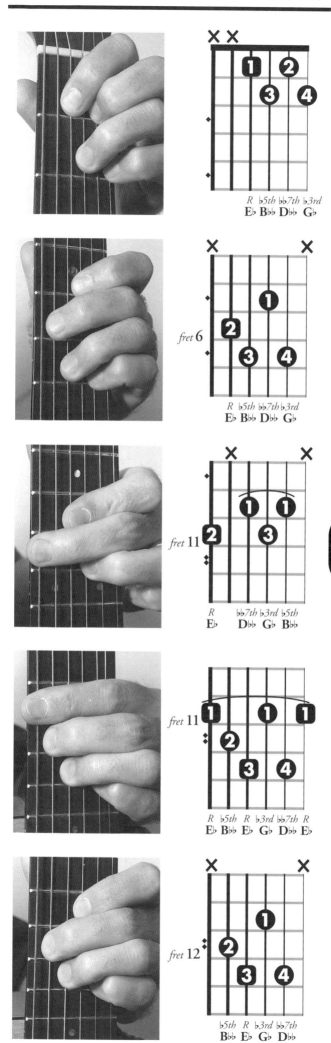

R ♭5th ♭♭7th ♭3rd
E♭ B♭♭ D♭♭ G♭

fret 6

R ♭5th ♭♭7th ♭3rd
E♭ B♭♭ D♭♭ G♭

fret 11

R ♭♭7th ♭3rd ♭5th
E♭ D♭♭ G♭ B♭♭

D♯
E♭

fret 11

R ♭5th R ♭3rd ♭♭7th R
E♭ B♭♭ E♭ G♭ D♭♭ E♭

fret 12

♭5th R ♭3rd ♭♭7th
B♭♭ E♭ G♭ D♭♭

E

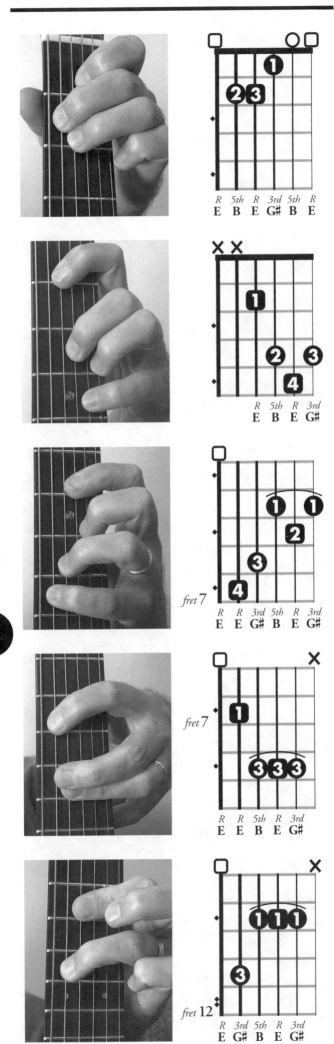

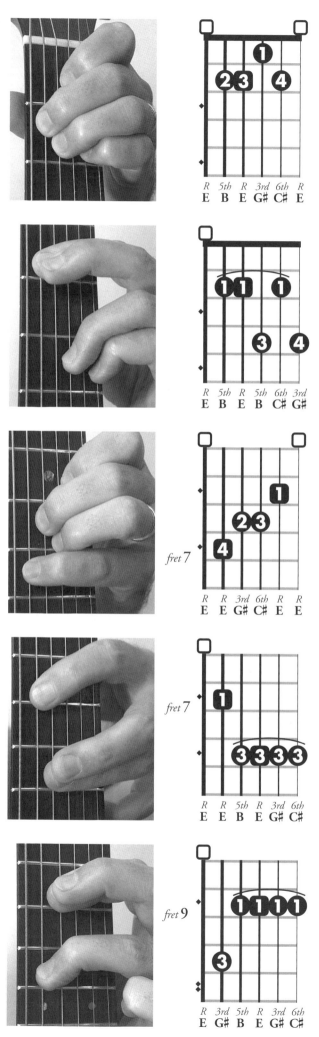

E

Emaj7

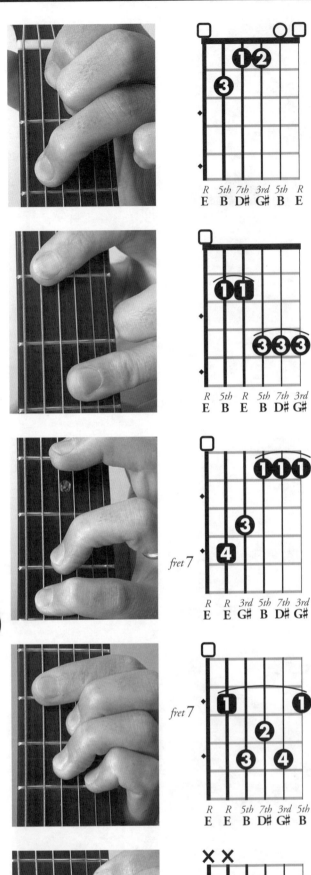

R	5th	7th	3rd	5th	R
E	B	D#	G#	B	E

R	5th	R	5th	7th	3rd
E	B	E	B	D#	G#

fret 7

R	R	3rd	5th	7th	3rd
E	E	G#	B	D#	G#

fret 7

R	R	5th	7th	3rd	5th
E	E	B	D#	G#	B

E

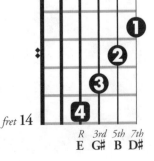

fret 14

R	3rd	5th	7th
E	G#	B	D#

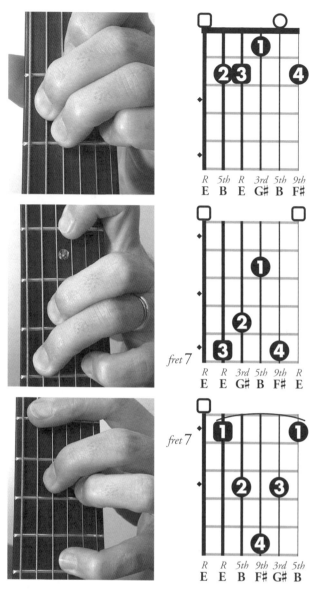

R	*5th*	*R*	*3rd*	*5th*	*9th*
E	**B**	**E**	**G#**	**B**	**F#**

fret 7

R	*R*	*3rd*	*5th*	*9th*	*R*
E	**E**	**G#**	**B**	**F#**	**E**

fret 7

R	*R*	*5th*	*9th*	*3rd*	*5th*
E	**E**	**B**	**F#**	**G#**	**B**

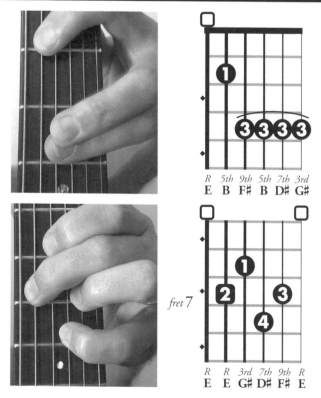

R	*5th*	*9th*	*5th*	*7th*	*3rd*
E	**B**	**F#**	**B**	**D#**	**G#**

fret 7

R	*R*	*3rd*	*7th*	*9th*	*R*
E	**E**	**G#**	**D#**	**F#**	**E**

Emaj7(♯11)

SCALE DEGREES: R 3rd 5th 7th ♯11th
CHORD TONES: E G♯ B D♯ A♯

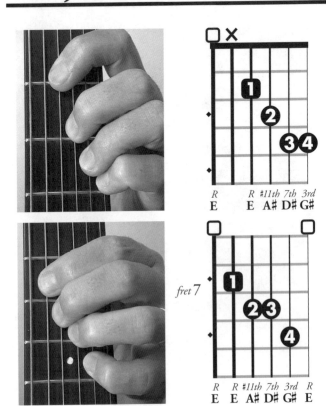

R   R ♯11th 7th 3rd
E   E A♯ D♯ G♯

fret 7

R R ♯11th 7th 3rd R
E E A♯ D♯ G♯ E

E6/9

SCALE DEGREES: R 3rd 5th 6th 9th
CHORD TONES: E G♯ B C♯ F♯

E

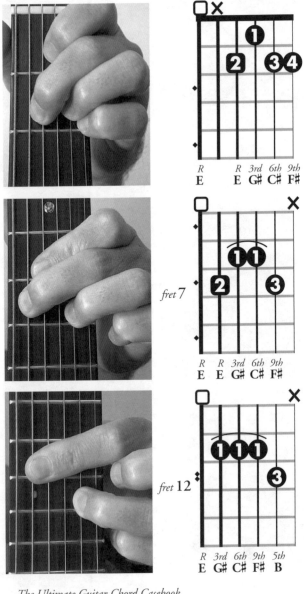

R   R 3rd 6th 9th
E   E G♯ C♯ F♯

fret 7

R R 3rd 6th 9th
E E G♯ C♯ F♯

fret 12

R 3rd 6th 9th 5th
E G♯ C♯ F♯ B

SCALE DEGREES: *R 2nd 5th*
CHORD TONES: E F# B

Esus2

R	5th	2nd	5th	5th	R
E	B	F#	B	B	E

fret 7

R	R	5th	R	2nd	5th
E	E	B	E	F#	B

SCALE DEGREES: *R 4th 5th*
CHORD TONES: E A B

Esus4

R	4th	R	4th	5th	R
E	A	E	A	B	E

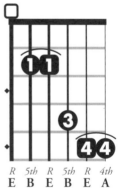

E

R	5th	R	5th	R	4th
E	B	E	B	E	A

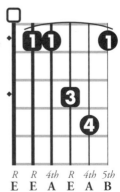

fret 7

R	R	4th	R	4th	5th
E	E	A	E	A	B

Em

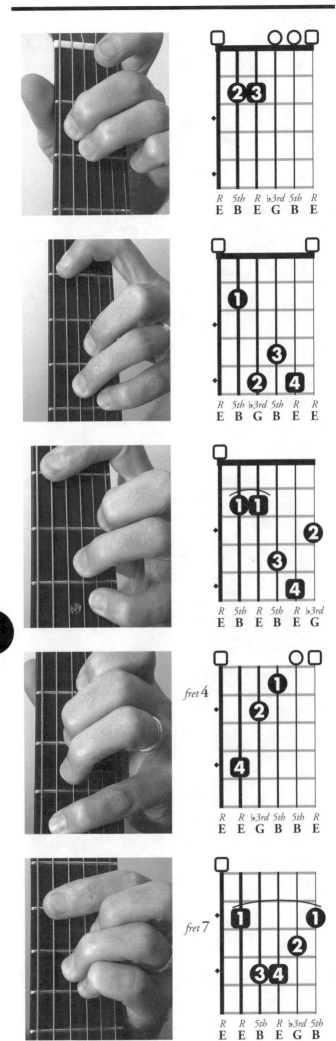

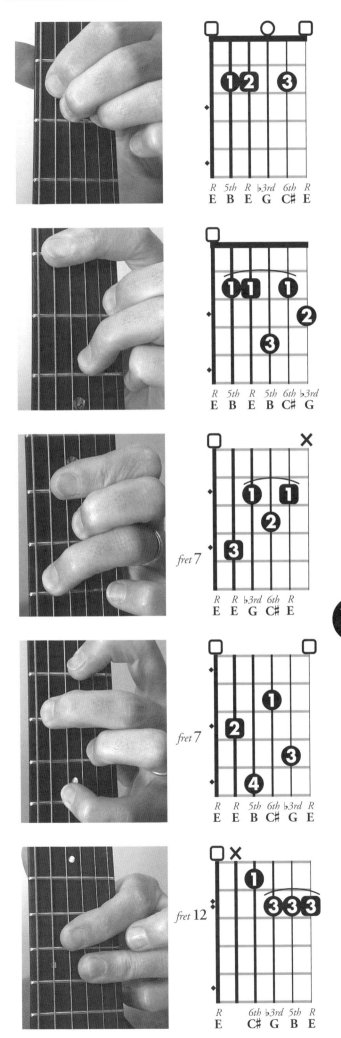

R 5th R ♭3rd 6th R
E B E G C♯ E

R 5th R 5th 6th ♭3rd
E B E B C♯ G

fret 7

R R ♭3rd 6th R
E E G C♯ E

fret 7

R R 5th 6th ♭3rd R
E E B C♯ G E

fret 12

R 6th ♭3rd 5th R
E C♯ G B E

Em7

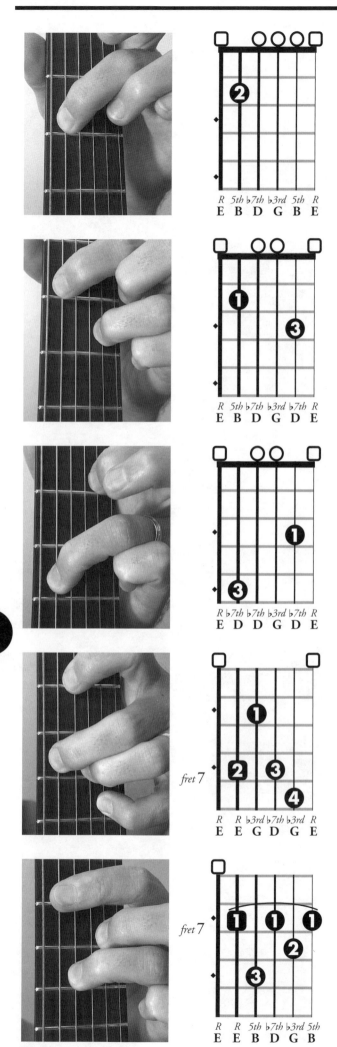

R 5th ♭7th ♭3rd 5th R
E B D G B E

R 5th ♭7th ♭3rd ♭7th R
E B D G D E

R ♭7th ♭7th ♭3rd ♭7th R
E D D G D E

fret 7

R R ♭3rd ♭7th ♭3rd R
E E G D G E

fret 7

R R 5th ♭7th ♭3rd 5th
E E B D G B

SCALE DEGREES: R ♭3rd ♭5th ♭7th
CHORD TONES: E G B♭ D

Em7(♭5)

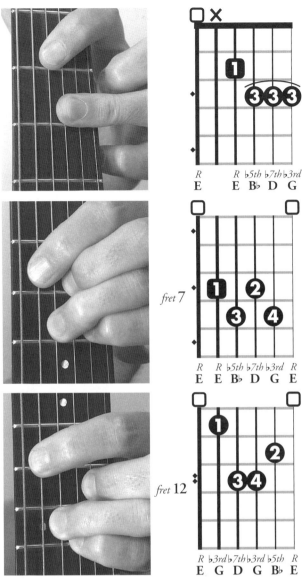

R   R ♭5th ♭7th ♭3rd
E   E   B♭   D   G

fret 7

R   R ♭5th ♭7th ♭3rd R
E   E   B♭   D   G   E

fret 12

R ♭3rd ♭7th ♭3rd ♭5th R
E   G   D   G   B♭   E

SCALE DEGREES: R ♭3rd 5th ♭7th 9th
CHORD TONES: E G B D F♯

Em9 **E**

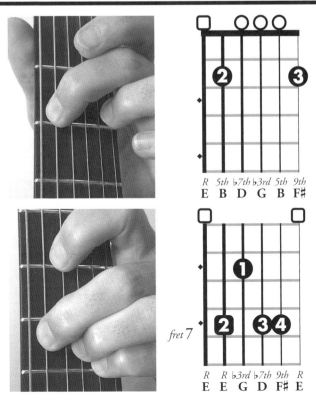

R   5th ♭7th ♭3rd 5th 9th
E   B   D   G   B   F♯

fret 7

R   R ♭3rd ♭7th 9th R
E   E   G   D   F♯   E

Em(maj7)

SCALE DEGREES:	R	♭3rd	5th	7th
CHORD TONES:	E	G	B	D♯

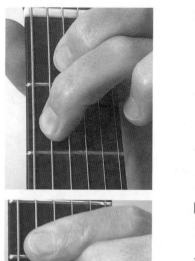

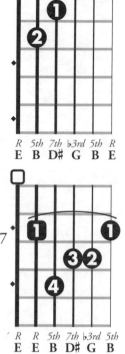

R	5th	7th	♭3rd	5th	R
E	B	D♯	G	B	E

fret 7

R	R	5th	7th	♭3rd	5th
E	E	B	D♯	G	B

Em(9)

SCALE DEGREES:	R	♭3rd	5th	9th
CHORD TONES:	E	G	B	F♯

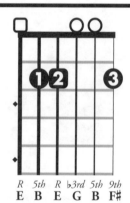

R	5th	R	♭3rd	5th	9th
E	B	E	G	B	F♯

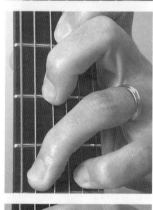

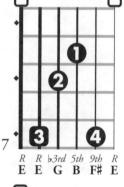

fret 7

R	R	♭3rd	5th	9th	R
E	E	G	B	F♯	E

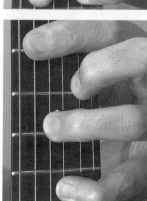

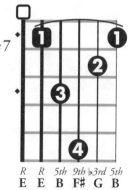

fret 7

R	R	5th	9th	♭3rd	5th
E	E	B	F♯	G	B

E

R 5th ♭7th 11th 5th ♭3rd
E   B   D   A   B   G

fret 7

R   R ♭3rd ♭7th 9th 11th
E   E   G   D   F#   A

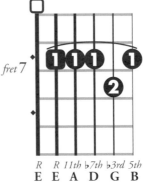

fret 7

R   R 11th ♭7th ♭3rd 5th
E   E   A   D   G   B

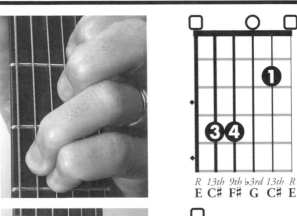

R 13th 9th ♭3rd 13th R
E C# F#   G   C#   E

fret 7

R   R 11th ♭7th ♭3rd 13th
E   E   A   D   G   C#

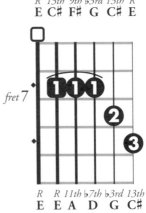

E7

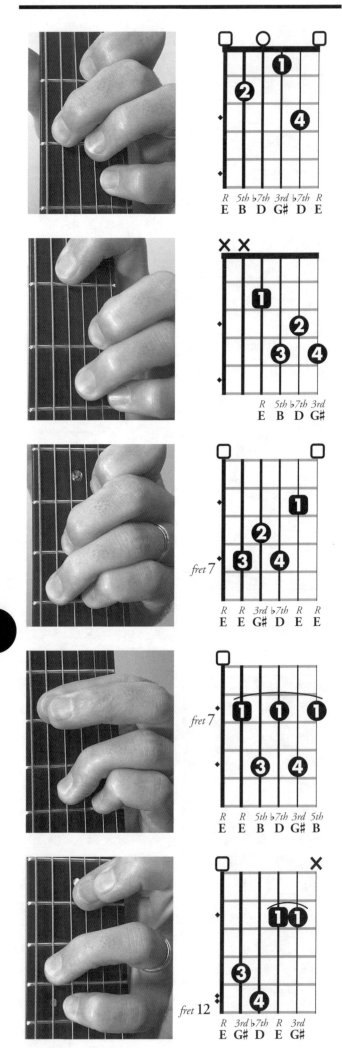

R 5th ♭7th 3rd ♭7th R
E   B   D   G#   D   E

R 5th ♭7th 3rd
E   B   D   G#

fret 7

R   R   3rd ♭7th R   R
E   E   G#   D   E   E

fret 7

R   R   5th ♭7th 3rd 5th
E   E   B   D   G#   B

fret 12

R   3rd ♭7th R   3rd
E   G#   D   E   G#

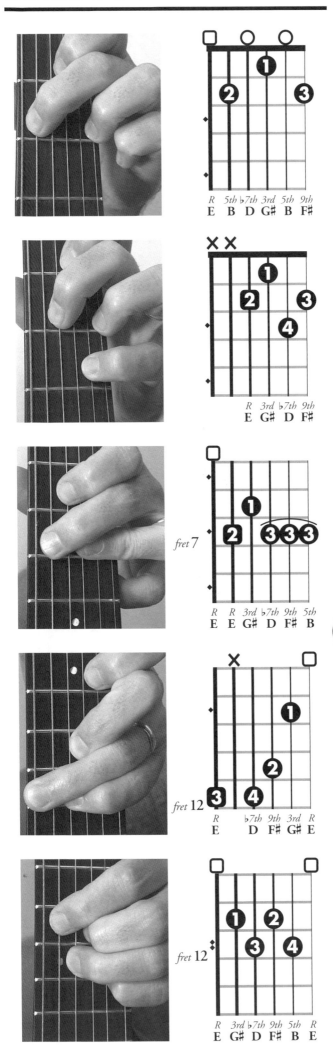

E7sus4

SCALE DEGREES: R 4th 5th ♭7th
CHORD TONES: E A B D

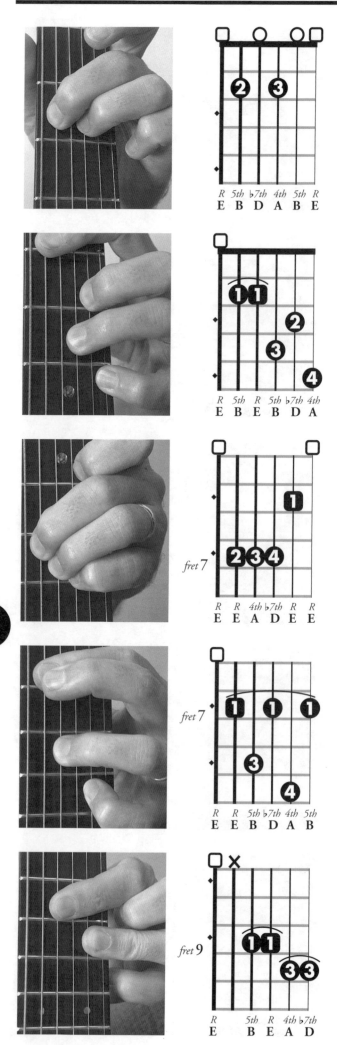

R 5th ♭7th 4th 5th R
E B D A B E

R 5th R 5th ♭7th 4th
E B E B D A

fret 7

R R 4th ♭7th R R
E E A D E E

fret 7

R R 5th ♭7th 4th 5th
E E B D A B

fret 9

R 5th R 4th ♭7th
E B E A D

E

SCALE DEGREES: *R 4th 5th ♭7th 9th*
CHORD TONES: E A B D F#

E9sus4

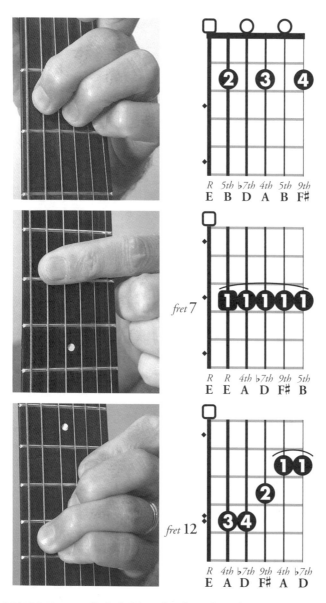

R 5th ♭7th 4th 5th 9th
E B D A B F#

fret 7

R R 4th ♭7th 9th 5th
E E A D F# B

fret 12

R 4th ♭7th 9th 4th ♭7th
E A D F# A D

SCALE DEGREES: *R 3rd 5th ♭7th 9th 11th 13th*
CHORD TONES: E G# B D F# A C#

E13   E

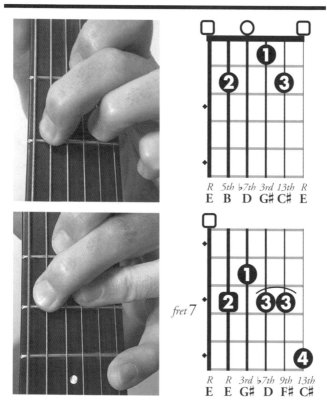

R 5th ♭7th 3rd 13th R
E B D G# C# E

fret 7

R R 3rd ♭7th 9th 13th
E E G# D F# C#

E7(♭5)

SCALE DEGREES: R 3rd ♭5th ♭7th
CHORD TONES: E G# B♭ D

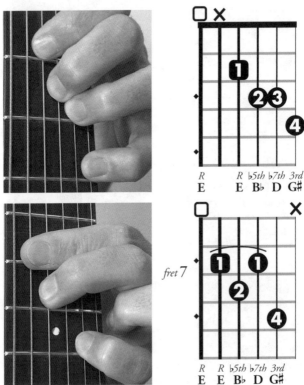

R		R	♭5th	♭7th	3rd
E		E	B♭	D	G#

fret 7

R	R	♭5th	♭7th	3rd
E	E	B♭	D	G#

E7(#5)

SCALE DEGREES: R 3rd #5th ♭7th
CHORD TONES: E G# B# D

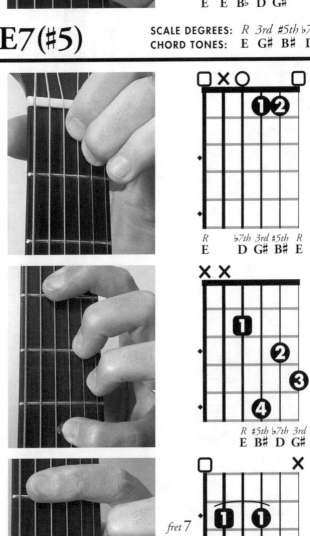

R		♭7th	3rd	#5th	R
E		D	G#	B#	E

R	#5th	♭7th	3rd
E	B#	D	G#

fret 7

R	R	#5th	♭7th	3rd
E	E	B#	D	G#

E7(♭9)

fret 7

fret 11

E7(♯9) E

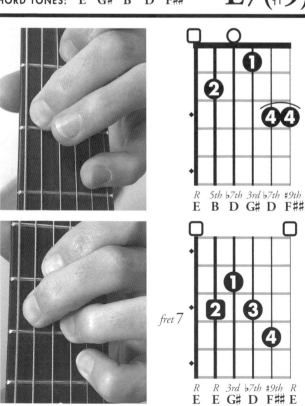

fret 7

E9(♭5)

SCALE DEGREES: R 3rd ♭5th ♭7th 9th
CHORD TONES: E G# B♭ D F#

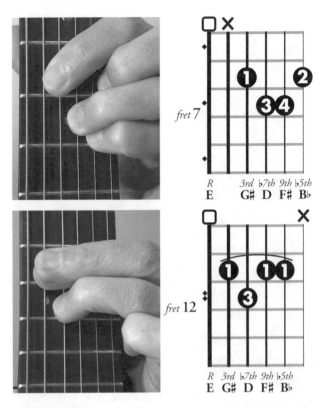

fret 7

R		3rd	♭7th	9th	♭5th
E		G#	D	F#	B♭

fret 12

R	3rd	♭7th	9th	♭5th
E	G#	D	F#	B♭

E9(#5)

SCALE DEGREES: R 3rd #5th ♭7th 9th
CHORD TONES: E G# B# D F#

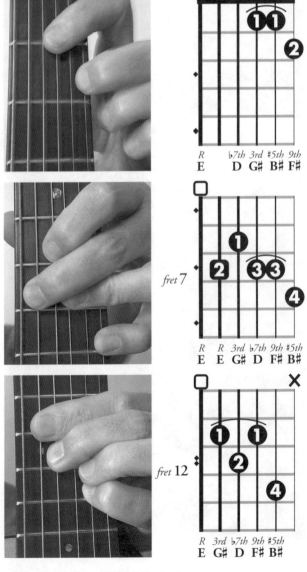

R		♭7th	3rd	#5th	9th
E		D	G#	B#	F#

fret 7

R	R	3rd	♭7th	9th	#5th
E	E	G#	D	F#	B#

fret 12

R	3rd	♭7th	9th	#5th
E	G#	D	F#	B#

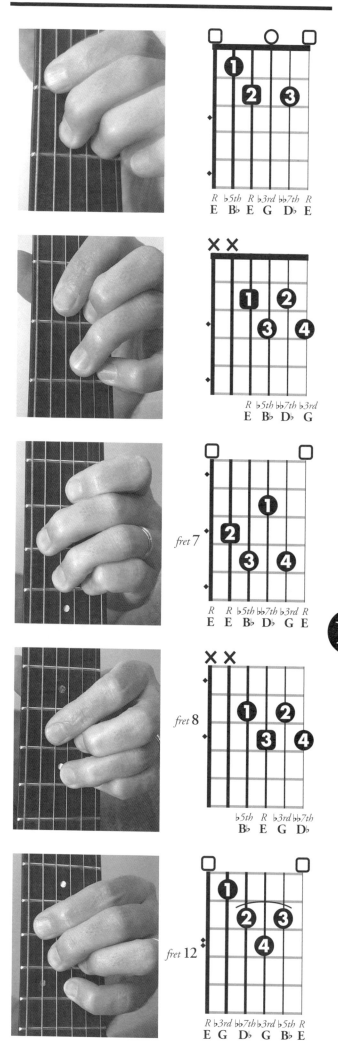

R	♭*5th*	*R*	♭*3rd*	♭♭*7th*	*R*
E	**B♭**	**E**	**G**	**D♭**	**E**

R	♭*5th*	♭♭*7th*	♭*3rd*
E	**B♭**	**D♭**	**G**

fret 7

R	*R*	♭*5th*	♭♭*7th*	♭*3rd*	*R*
E	**E**	**B♭**	**D♭**	**G**	**E**

fret 8

♭*5th*	*R*	♭*3rd*	♭♭*7th*
B♭	**E**	**G**	**D♭**

fret 12

R	♭*3rd*	♭♭*7th*	♭*3rd*	♭*5th*	*R*
E	**G**	**D♭**	**G**	**B♭**	**E**

E

F

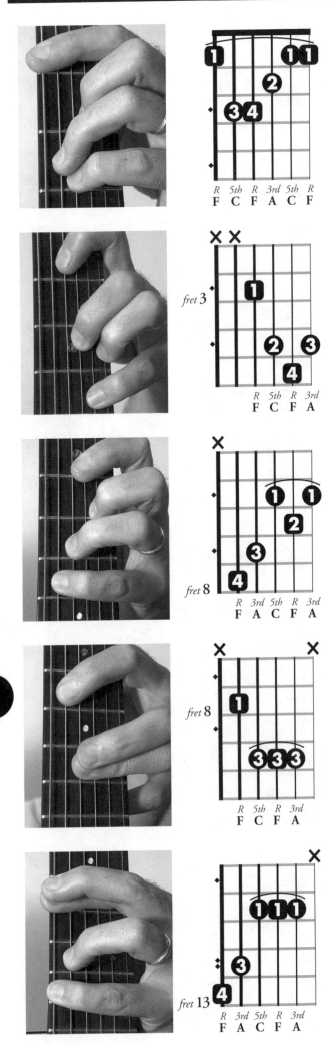

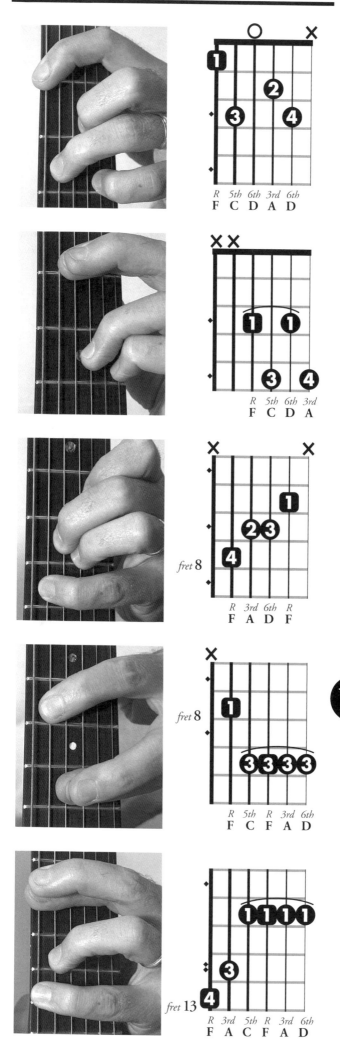

F

Fmaj7

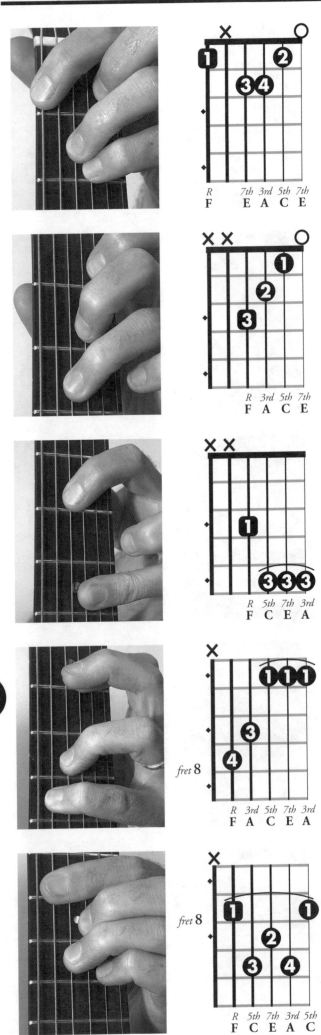

F

SCALE DEGREES: R 3rd 5th 9th
CHORD TONES: F A C G

F(9)

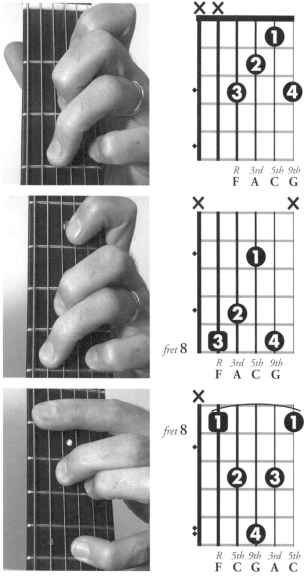

R 3rd 5th 9th
F A C G

fret 8

R 3rd 5th 9th
F A C G

fret 8

R 5th 9th 3rd 5th
F C G A C

SCALE DEGREES: R 3rd 5th 7th 9th
CHORD TONES: F A C E G

Fmaj9

F

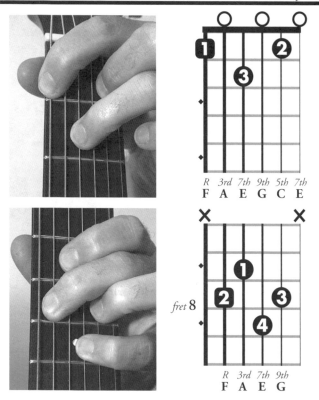

R 3rd 7th 9th 5th 7th
F A E G C E

fret 8

R 3rd 7th 9th
F A E G

Fmaj7(#11)

SCALE DEGREES: *R 3rd 5th 7th #11th*
CHORD TONES: F A C E B

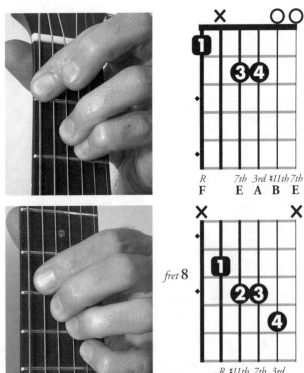

R		7th	3rd	#11th	7th
F		E	A	B	E

fret 8

	R	#11th	7th	3rd	
	F	B	E	A	

F6/9

SCALE DEGREES: *R 3rd 5th 6th 9th*
CHORD TONES: F A C D G

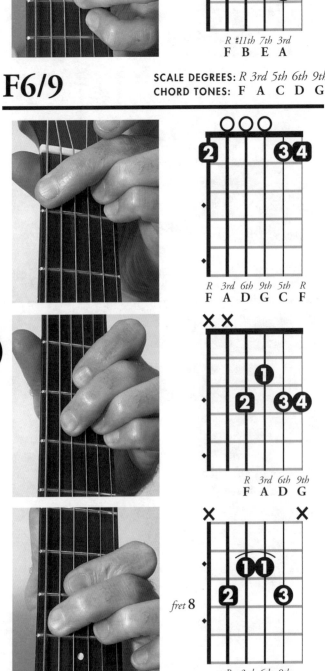

R	3rd	6th	9th	5th	R
F	A	D	G	C	F

	R	3rd	6th	9th	
	F	A	D	G	

fret 8

	R	3rd	6th	9th	
	F	A	D	G	

F

SCALE DEGREES: *R 2nd 5th*
CHORD TONES: F G C

Fsus2

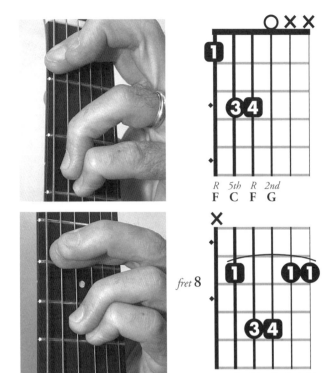

R	5th	R	2nd
F	C	F	G

R	5th	R	2nd	5th
F	C	F	G	C

fret 8

SCALE DEGREES: *R 4th 5th*
CHORD TONES: F B♭ C

Fsus4

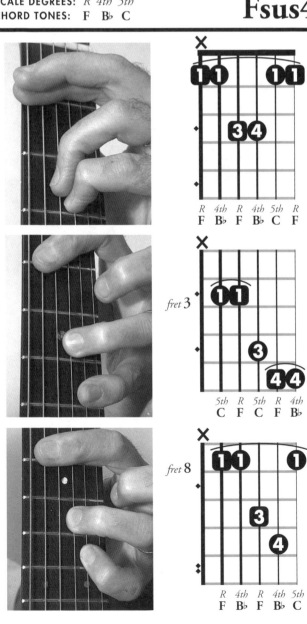

R	4th	R	4th	5th	R
F	B♭	F	B♭	C	F

fret 3

5th	R	5th	R	4th
C	F	C	F	B♭

fret 8

R	4th	R	4th	5th
F	B♭	F	B♭	C

F

Fm

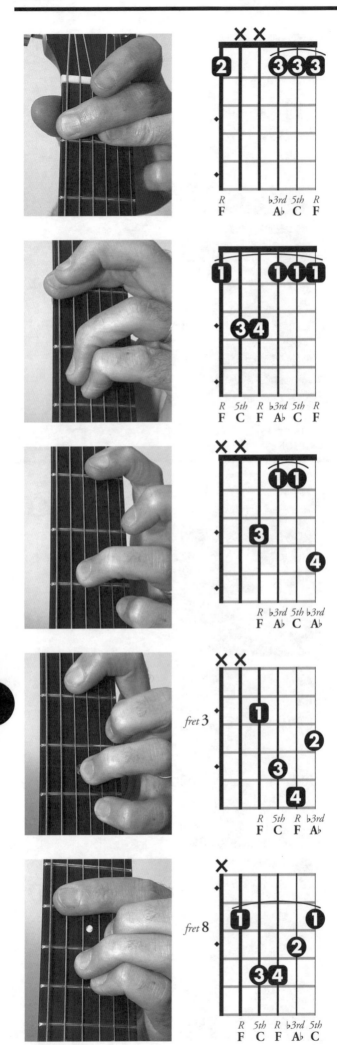

× ×

2   3 3 3

R   ♭3rd 5th R
F   A♭ C F

1   1 1 1

3 4

R 5th R ♭3rd 5th R
F C F A♭ C F

× ×

1 1

3

4

R ♭3rd 5th ♭3rd
F A♭ C A♭

× ×

fret 3

1

2

3

4

R 5th R ♭3rd
F C F A♭

×

fret 8

1   1

2

3 4

R 5th R ♭3rd 5th
F C F A♭ C

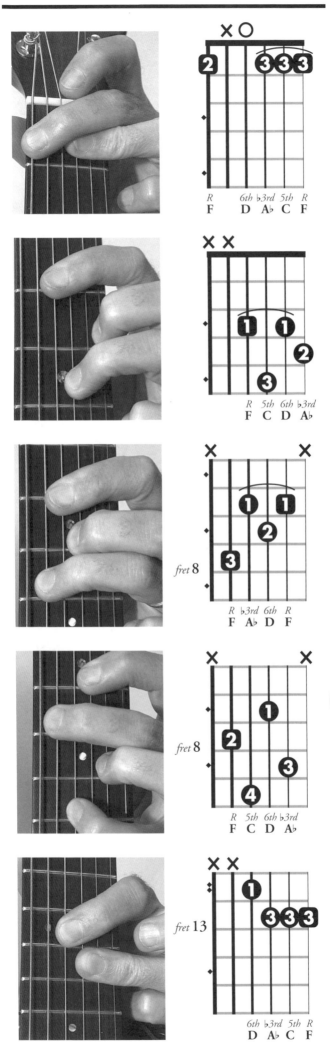

fret 8

fret 8

fret 13

F

Fm7

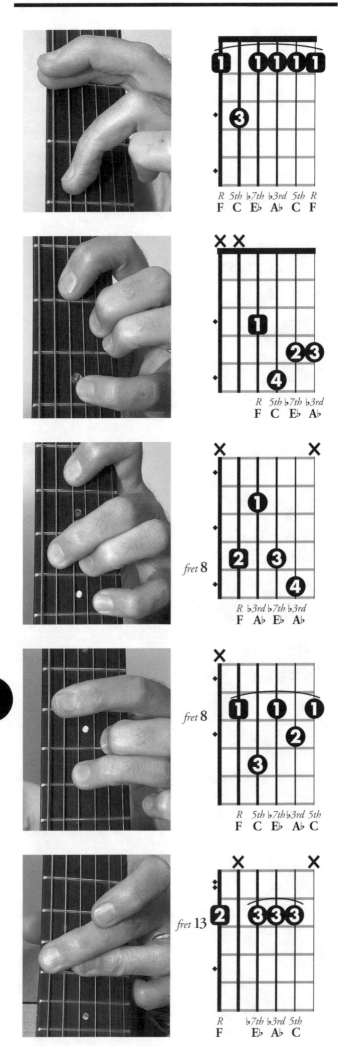

R 5th ♭7th ♭3rd 5th R
F C E♭ A♭ C F

R 5th ♭7th ♭3rd
F C E♭ A♭

fret 8

R ♭3rd ♭7th ♭3rd
F A♭ E♭ A♭

fret 8

R 5th ♭7th ♭3rd 5th
F C E♭ A♭ C

fret 13

R ♭7th ♭3rd 5th
F E♭ A♭ C

F

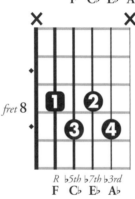

R   ♭7th ♭3rd ♭5th
F   E♭   A♭   C♭

R ♭5th ♭7th ♭3rd
F C♭ E♭ A♭

fret 8

R ♭5th ♭7th ♭3rd
F C♭ E♭ A♭

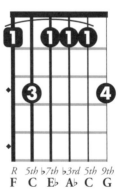

F

R 5th ♭7th ♭3rd 5th 9th
F C E♭ A♭ C G

fret 8

R ♭3rd ♭7th 9th
F A♭ E♭ G

Fm(maj7)

SCALE DEGREES: R ♭3rd 5th 7th
CHORD TONES: F A♭ C E

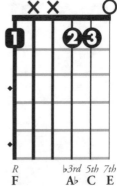

R   ♭3rd 5th 7th
F   A♭ C E

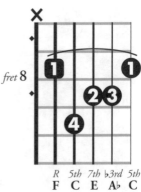

fret 8

R   5th 7th ♭3rd 5th
F   C   E   A♭   C

Fm(9)

SCALE DEGREES: R ♭3rd 5th 9th
CHORD TONES: F A♭ C G

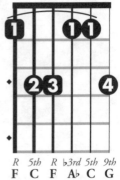

R 5th R ♭3rd 5th 9th
F C F A♭ C G

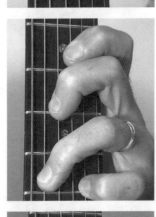
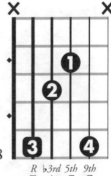

fret 8

R ♭3rd 5th 9th
F A♭ C G

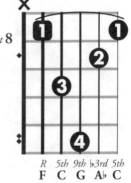

fret 8

R 5th 9th ♭3rd 5th
F C G A♭ C

F

Fm11

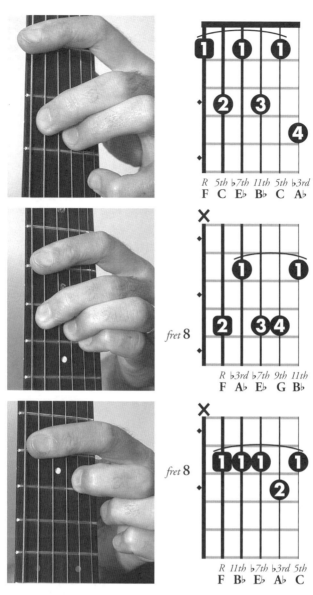

R 5th ♭7th 11th 5th ♭3rd
F C E♭ B♭ C A♭

fret 8

R ♭3rd ♭7th 9th 11th
F A♭ E♭ G B♭

fret 8

R 11th ♭7th ♭3rd 5th
F B♭ E♭ A♭ C

Fm13

F

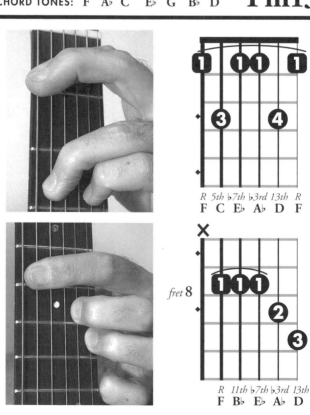

R 5th ♭7th ♭3rd 13th R
F C E♭ A♭ D F

fret 8

R 11th ♭7th ♭3rd 13th
F B♭ E♭ A♭ D

F7

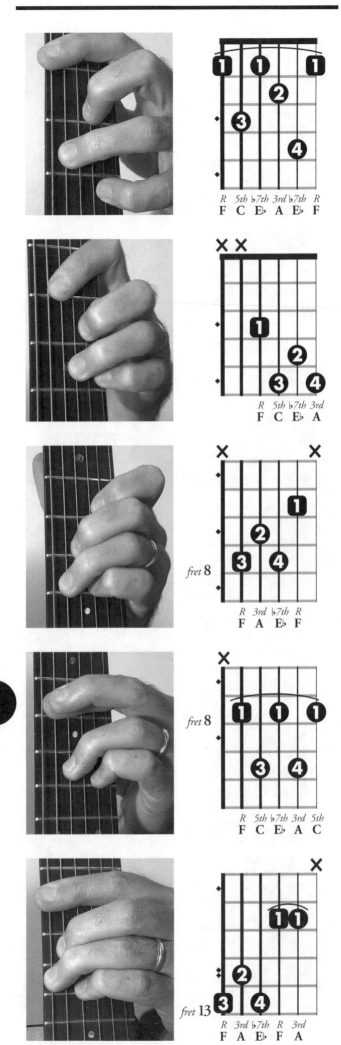

R 5th ♭7th 3rd ♭7th R
F C E♭ A E♭ F

R 5th ♭7th 3rd
F C E♭ A

fret 8

R 3rd ♭7th R
F A E♭ F

fret 8

R 5th ♭7th 3rd 5th
F C E♭ A C

fret 13

R 3rd ♭7th R 3rd
F A E♭ F A

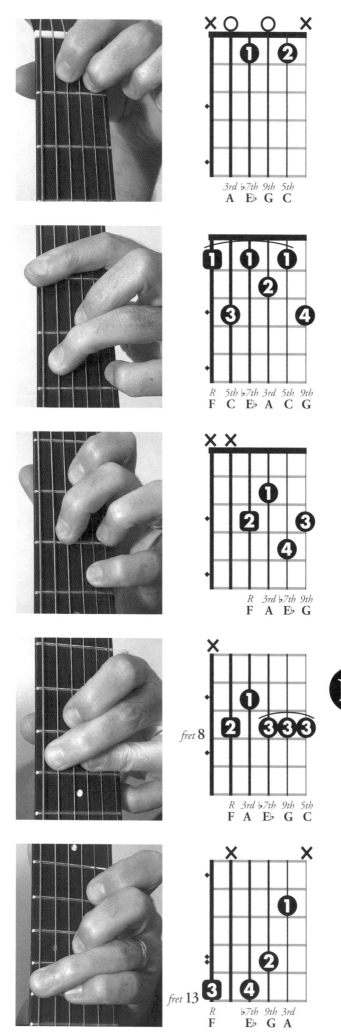

3rd ♭7th 9th 5th
A E♭ G C

R 5th ♭7th 3rd 5th 9th
F C E♭ A C G

R 3rd ♭7th 9th
F A E♭ G

fret 8

R 3rd ♭7th 9th 5th
F A E♭ G C

fret 13

R   ♭7th 9th 3rd
F   E♭ G A

F

F7sus4

R   5th ♭7th 4th 5th R
F   C   E♭   B♭   C   F

fret 3

R   5th ♭7th 4th
F   C   E♭   B♭

fret 8

R   4th ♭7th R
F   B♭   E♭   F

fret 8

R   5th ♭7th 4th 5th
F   C   E♭   B♭   C

fret 10

5th R   4th ♭7th
C   F   B♭   E♭

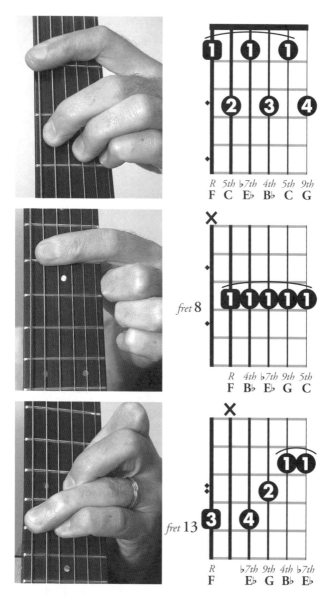

R 5th ♭7th 4th 5th 9th
F C E♭ B♭ C G

fret 8

R 4th ♭7th 9th 5th
F B♭ E♭ G C

fret 13

R ♭7th 9th 4th ♭7th
F E♭ G B♭ E♭

SCALE DEGREES: *R 3rd 5th ♭7th 9th 11th 13th*
CHORD TONES: F A C E♭ G B♭ D

F13

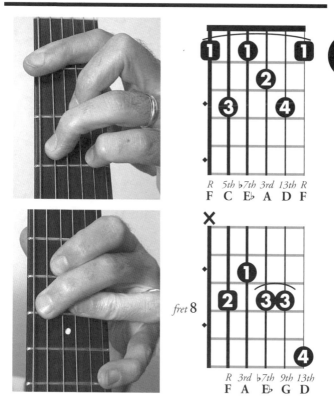

R 5th ♭7th 3rd 13th R
F C E♭ A D F

fret 8

R 3rd ♭7th 9th 13th
F A E♭ G D

F

F7(♭5)

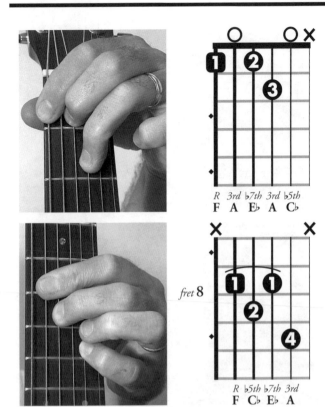

R 3rd ♭7th 3rd ♭5th
F A E♭ A C♭

fret 8

R ♭5th ♭7th 3rd
F C♭ E♭ A

F7(♯5)

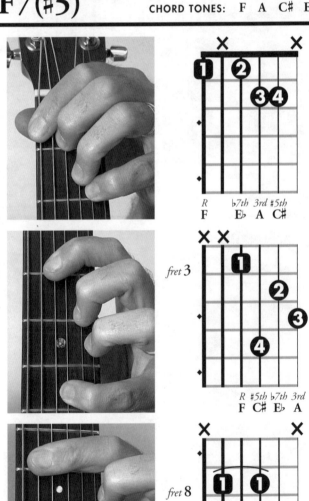

R ♭7th 3rd ♯5th
F E♭ A C♯

fret 3

R ♯5th ♭7th 3rd
F C♯ E♭ A

fret 8

R ♯5th ♭7th 3rd
F C♯ E♭ A

F

SCALE DEGREES: *R 3rd 5th ♭7th ♭9th*
CHORD TONES: F A C E♭ G♭

F7(♭9)

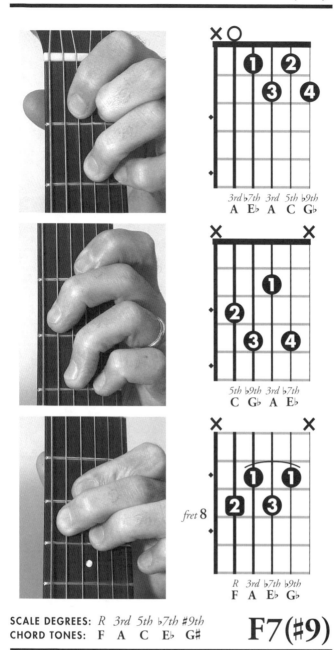

3rd ♭7th 3rd 5th ♭9th
A E♭ A C G♭

5th ♭9th 3rd ♭7th
C G♭ A E♭

fret 8

R 3rd ♭7th ♭9th
F A E♭ G♭

SCALE DEGREES: *R 3rd 5th ♭7th ♯9th*
CHORD TONES: F A C E♭ G♯

F7(♯9)

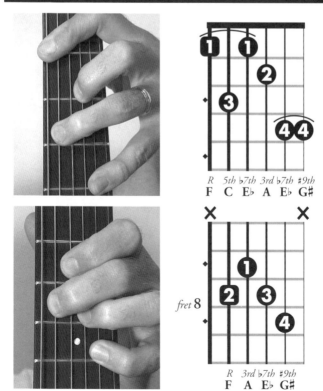

R 5th ♭7th 3rd ♭7th ♯9th
F C E♭ A E♭ G♯

fret 8

R 3rd ♭7th ♯9th
F A E♭ G♯

F9(♭5)

SCALE DEGREES: R 3rd ♭5th ♭7th 9th
CHORD TONES: F A C♭ E♭ G

R   3rd ♭7th 9th ♭5th
F   A   E♭   G   C♭

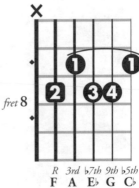

fret 8

R   3rd ♭7th 9th ♭5th
F   A   E♭   G   C♭

F9(♯5)

SCALE DEGREES: R 3rd ♯5th ♭7th 9th
CHORD TONES: F A C♯ E♭ G

R   3rd ♭7th 9th ♯5th
F   A   E♭   G   C♯

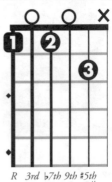

3rd ♭7th 3rd ♯5th 9th
A   E♭   A   C♯   G

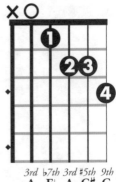

fret 8

R   3rd ♭7th 9th ♯5th
F   A   E♭   G   C♯

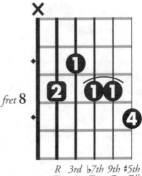

F

Fdim7

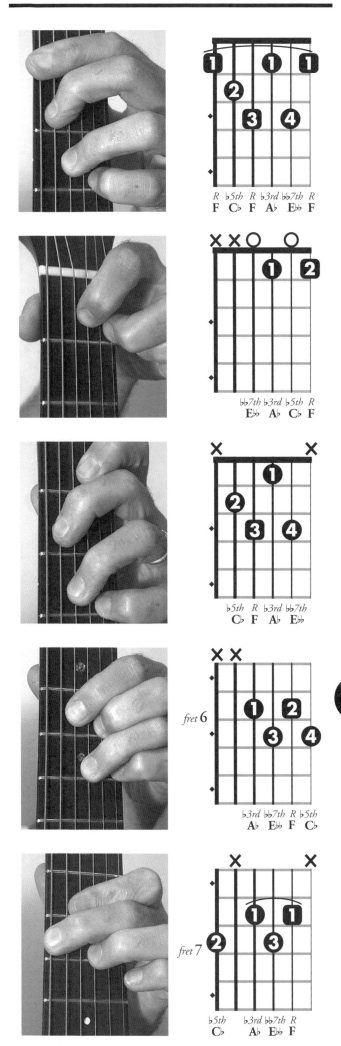

R   b5th   R   b3rd bb7th R
F   Cb   F   Ab   Ebb   F

bb7th b3rd b5th R
Ebb   Ab   Cb   F

b5th   R   b3rd bb7th
Cb   F   Ab   Ebb

fret 6

b3rd bb7th R b5th
Ab   Ebb   F   Cb

F

fret 7

b5th   b3rd bb7th R
Cb   Ab   Ebb   F

F#

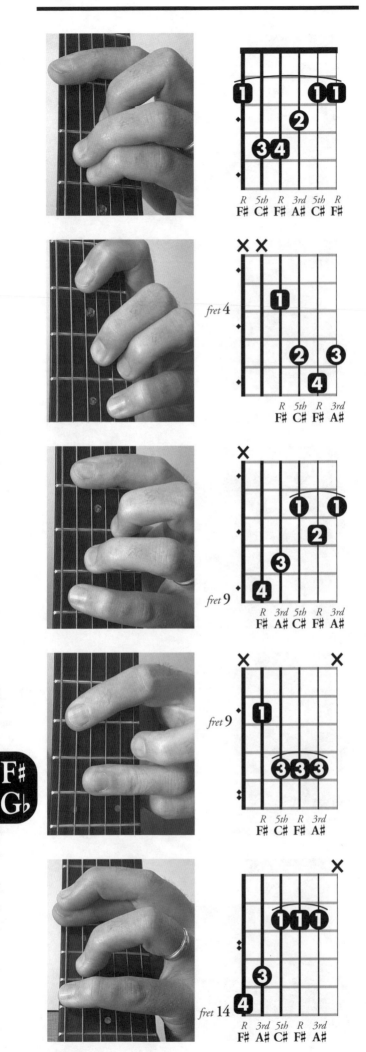

R 5th R 3rd 5th R
F# C# F# A# C# F#

fret 4

R 5th R 3rd
F# C# F# A#

fret 9

R 3rd 5th R 3rd
F# A# C# F# A#

fret 9

R 5th R 3rd
F# C# F# A#

fret 14

R 3rd 5th R 3rd
F# A# C# F# A#

F#
Gb

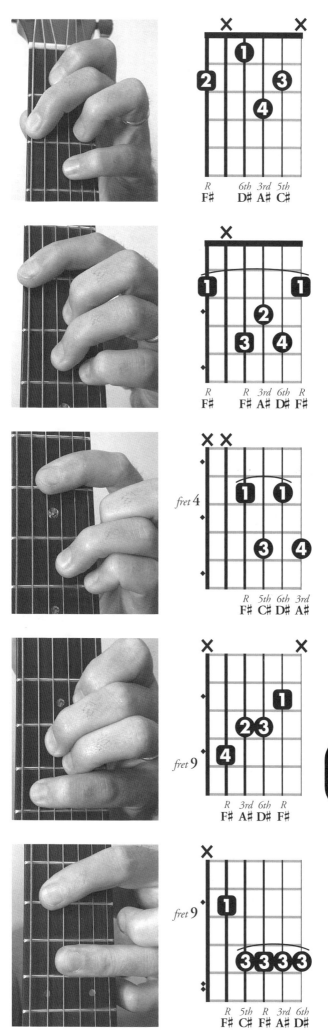

R   6th   3rd 5th
F♯   D♯   A♯   C♯

R   R   3rd   6th   R
F♯   F♯ A♯   D♯   F♯

fret 4

R   5th   6th   3rd
F♯   C♯   D♯   A♯

fret 9

R   3rd   6th   R
F♯   A♯   D♯   F♯

F♯
G♭

fret 9

R   5th   R   3rd   6th
F♯   C♯   F♯   A♯   D♯

F#maj7

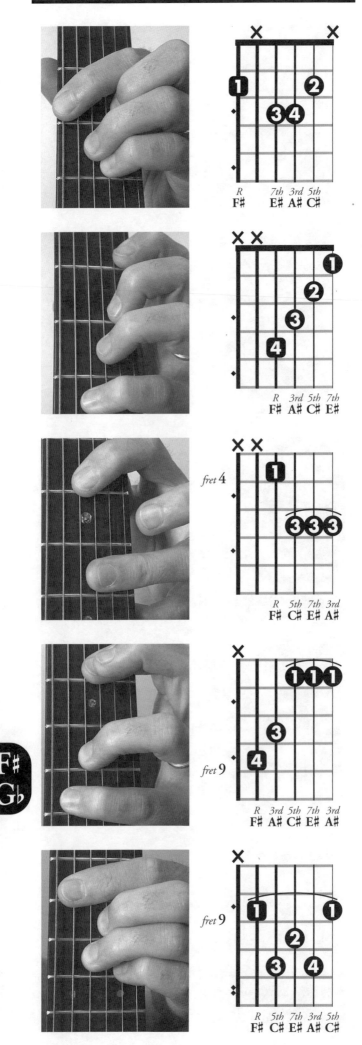

R   7th 3rd 5th
F#   E# A# C#

R 3rd 5th 7th
F# A# C# E#

fret 4

R 5th 7th 3rd
F# C# E# A#

fret 9

R 3rd 5th 7th 3rd
F# A# C# E# A#

fret 9

R 5th 7th 3rd 5th
F# C# E# A# C#

F#
Gb

F#(9)

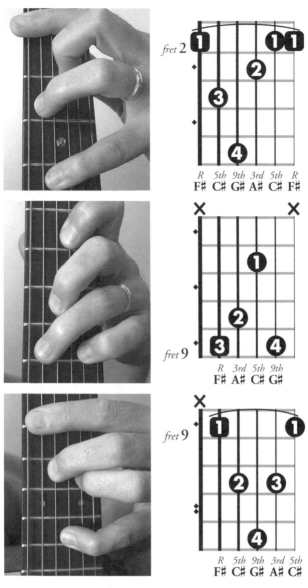

F#maj9

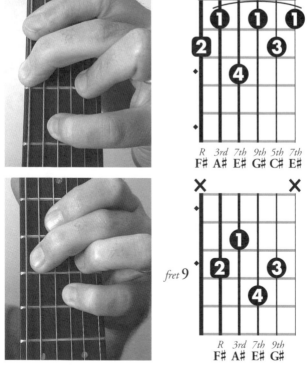

F#
Gb

F#maj7(#11)

SCALE DEGREES: *R 3rd 5th 7th #11th*
CHORD TONES: F# A# C# E# B#

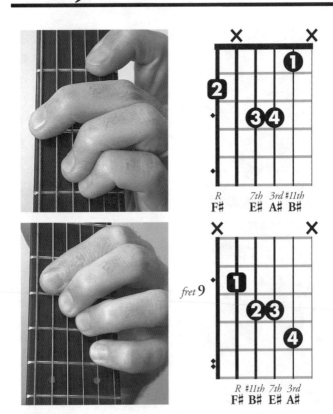

R   7th 3rd #11th
F#   E#   A#   B#

fret 9

R   #11th 7th 3rd
F# B#   E#   A#

F#6/9

SCALE DEGREES: *R 3rd 5th 6th 9th*
CHORD TONES: F# A# C# D# G#

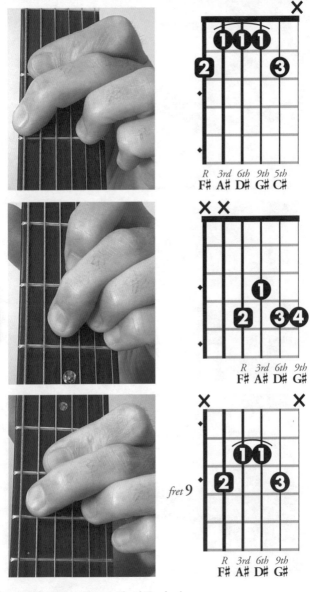

R   3rd 6th 9th 5th
F# A#   D#   G#   C#

R   3rd 6th 9th
F# A#   D#   G#

fret 9

R   3rd 6th 9th
F# A#   D#   G#

F#
Gb

F♯sus2

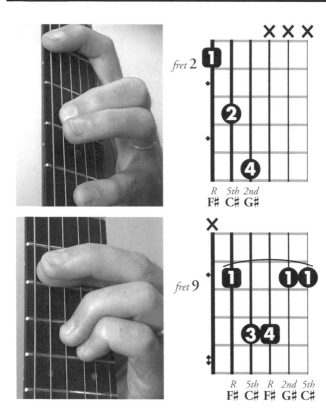

fret 2

R	5th	2nd
F♯	C♯	G♯

fret 9

R	5th	R	2nd	5th
F♯	C♯	F♯	G♯	C♯

F♯sus4

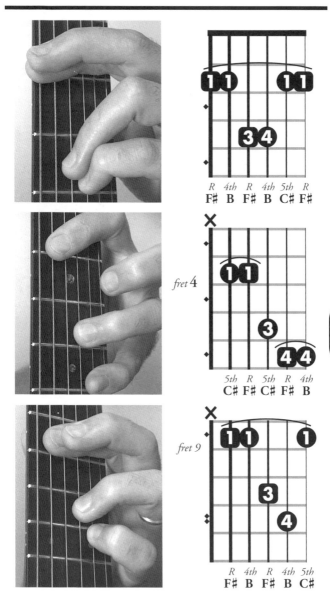

R	4th	R	4th	5th	R
F♯	B	F♯	B	C♯	F♯

fret 4

5th	R	5th	R	4th
C♯	F♯	C♯	F♯	B

F♯
G♭

fret 9

R	4th	R	4th	5th
F♯	B	F♯	B	C♯

F#m

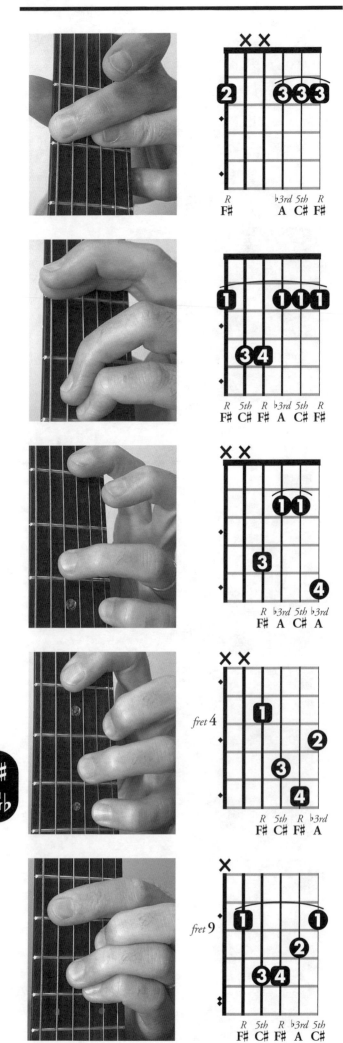

R   ♭3rd 5th R
F#   A C# F#

R 5th R ♭3rd 5th R
F# C# F# A C# F#

R ♭3rd 5th ♭3rd
F# A C# A

fret 4

R 5th R ♭3rd
F# C# F# A

fret 9

R 5th R ♭3rd 5th
F# C# F# A C#

F#
G♭

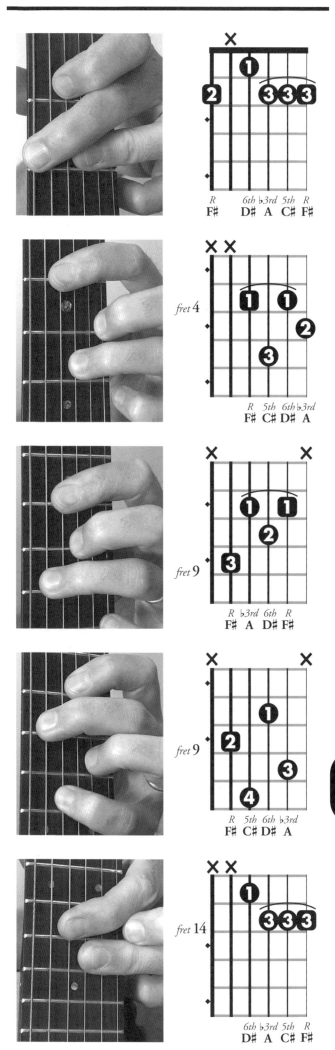

F#m7

SCALE DEGREES: R ♭3rd 5th ♭7th
CHORD TONES: F# A C# E

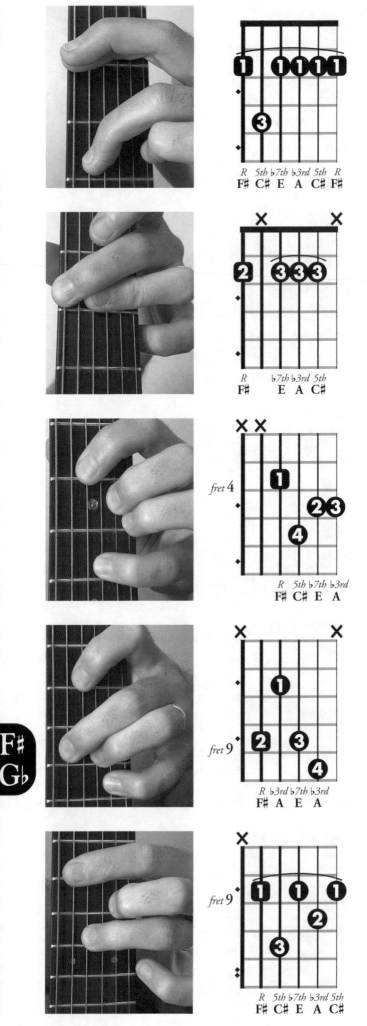

R 5th ♭7th ♭3rd 5th R
F# C# E A C# F#

R ♭7th ♭3rd 5th
F# E A C#

fret 4

R 5th ♭7th ♭3rd
F# C# E A

fret 9

R ♭3rd ♭7th ♭3rd
F# A E A

F#
G♭

fret 9

R 5th ♭7th ♭3rd 5th
F# C# E A C#

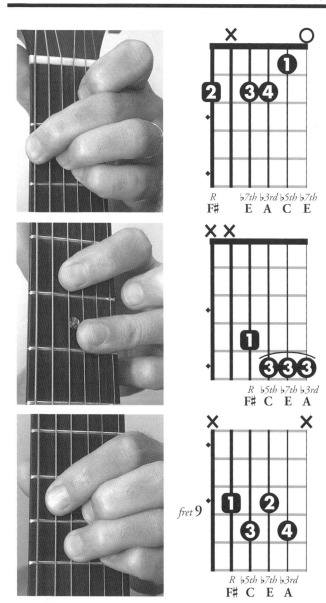

R   ♭7th ♭3rd ♭5th ♭7th
F#   E   A   C   E

R ♭5th ♭7th ♭3rd
F# C   E   A

R ♭5th ♭7th ♭3rd
F# C   E   A

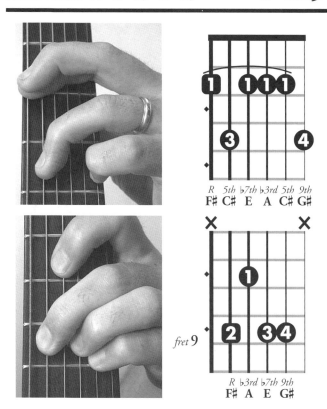

R   5th ♭7th ♭3rd 5th 9th
F# C#   E   A   C# G#

F#
G♭

R ♭3rd ♭7th 9th
F# A   E   G#

F#m(maj7)

SCALE DEGREES: R ♭3rd 5th 7th
CHORD TONES: F# A C# E#

×

R 5th 7th ♭3rd 5th
F# C# E# A C#

×

fret 9

R 5th 7th ♭3rd 5th
F# C# E# A C#

F#m(9)

SCALE DEGREES: R ♭3rd 5th 9th
CHORD TONES: F# A C# G#

R 5th R ♭3rd 5th 9th
F# C# F# A C# G#

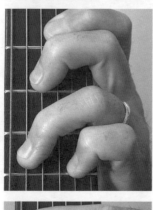
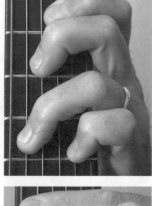

× ×

fret 9

R ♭3rd 5th 9th
F# A C# G#

×

fret 9

R 5th 9th ♭3rd 5th
F# C# G# A C#

F#
G♭

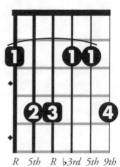
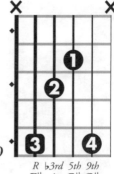
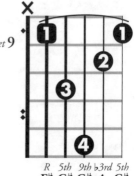

F♯m11

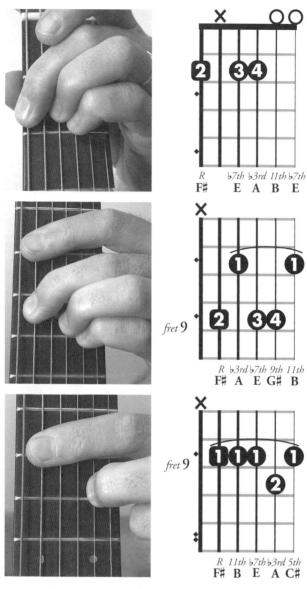

F♯m13

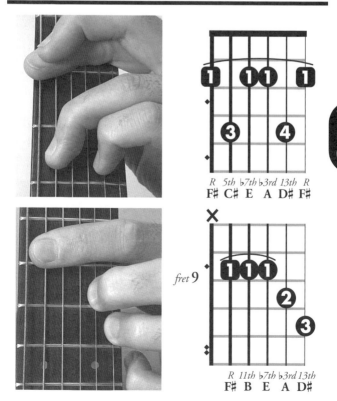

F♯
G♭

F#7

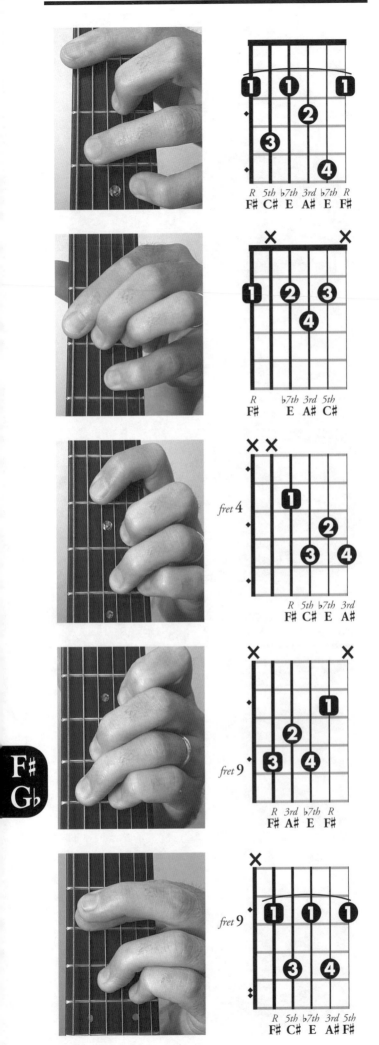

R 5th ♭7th 3rd ♭7th R
F# C# E A# E F#

R ♭7th 3rd 5th
F# E A# C#

fret 4

R 5th ♭7th 3rd
F# C# E A#

F#
G♭

fret 9

R 3rd ♭7th R
F# A# E F#

fret 9

R 5th ♭7th 3rd 5th
F# C# E A# F#

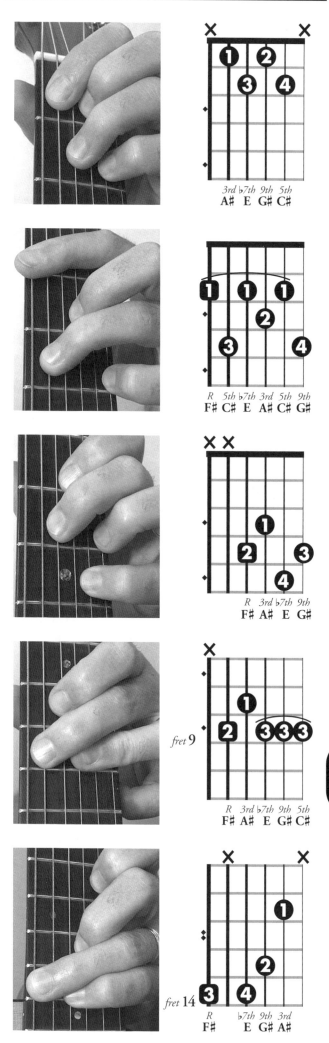

×   ×

3rd b7th 9th 5th
A# E G# C#

R 5th b7th 3rd 5th 9th
F# C# E A# C# G#

× ×

R 3rd b7th 9th
F# A# E G#

fret 9

R 3rd b7th 9th 5th
F# A# E G# C#

**F#
Gb**

×   ×

fret 14

R b7th 9th 3rd
F# E G# A#

F#7sus4

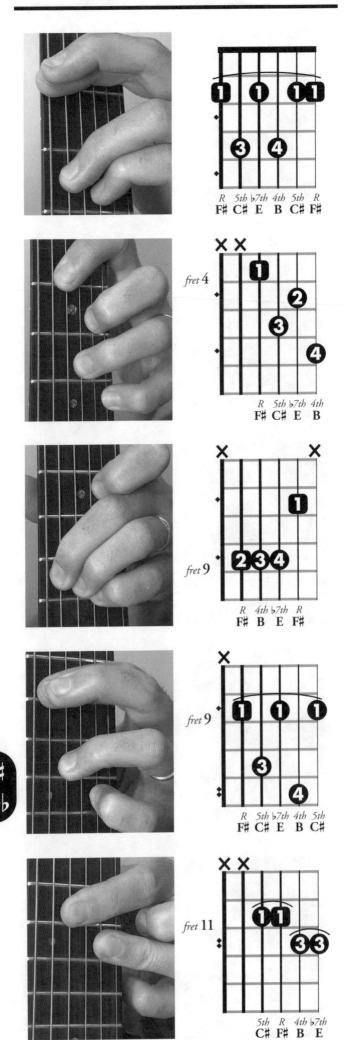

R 5th ♭7th 4th 5th R
F# C# E B C# F#

fret 4

R 5th ♭7th 4th
F# C# E B

fret 9

R 4th ♭7th R
F# B E F#

fret 9

R 5th ♭7th 4th 5th
F# C# E B C#

F#
G♭

fret 11

5th R 4th ♭7th
C# F# B E

SCALE DEGREES: *R 4th 5th ♭7th 9th*
CHORD TONES: **F♯ B C♯ E G♯**

F♯9sus4

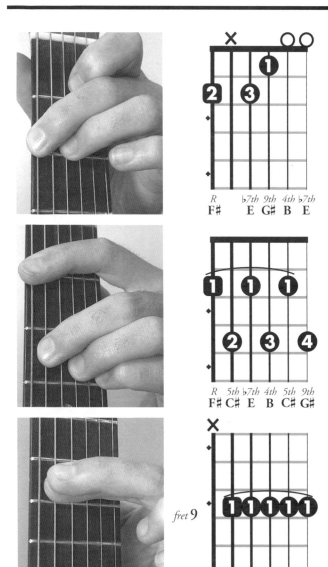

R · ♭7th 9th 4th ♭7th
F♯ · E G♯ B E

R 5th ♭7th 4th 5th 9th
F♯ C♯ E B C♯ G♯

fret 9

R 4th ♭7th 9th 5th
F♯ B E G♯ C♯

SCALE DEGREES: *R 3rd 5th ♭7th 9th 11th 13th*
CHORD TONES: **F♯ A♯ C♯ E G♯ B D♯**

F♯13

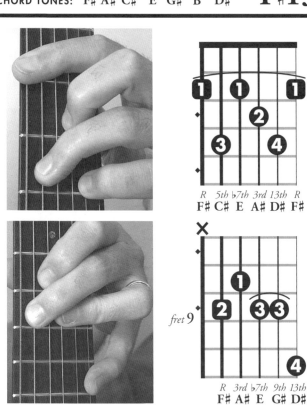

R 5th ♭7th 3rd 13th R
F♯ C♯ E A♯ D♯ F♯

fret 9

R 3rd ♭7th 9th 13th
F♯ A♯ E G♯ D♯

**F♯
G♭**

F#7(♭5)

SCALE DEGREES: R 3rd ♭5th ♭7th
CHORD TONES: F# A# C E

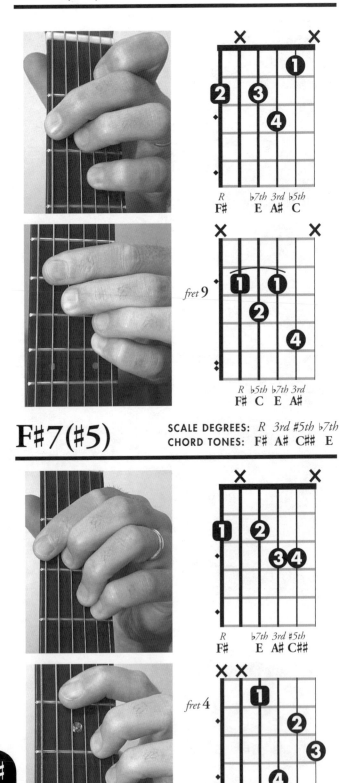

R   ♭7th 3rd ♭5th
F#   E   A#   C

fret 9

R ♭5th ♭7th 3rd
F# C   E   A#

F#7(#5)

SCALE DEGREES: R 3rd #5th ♭7th
CHORD TONES: F# A# C## E

R   ♭7th 3rd #5th
F#   E   A# C##

fret 4

R #5th ♭7th 3rd
F# C## E   A#

fret 9

R #5th ♭7th 3rd
F# C## E   A#

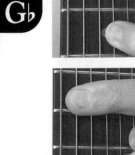

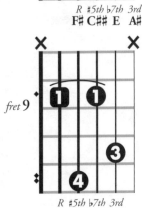

SCALE DEGREES: *R 3rd 5th ♭7th ♭9th*
CHORD TONES: F# A# C# E G

F#7(♭9)

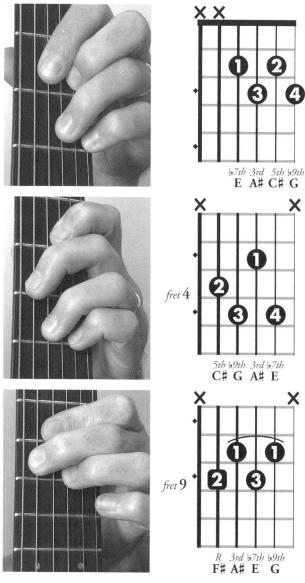

♭7th 3rd 5th ♭9th
E A# C# G

fret 4

5th ♭9th 3rd ♭7th
C# G A# E

fret 9

R 3rd ♭7th ♭9th
F# A# E G

SCALE DEGREES: *R 3rd 5th ♭7th #9th*
CHORD TONES: F# A# C# E G##

F#7(#9)

F#
G♭

R 5th ♭7th 3rd ♭7th #9th
F# C# E A# E G##

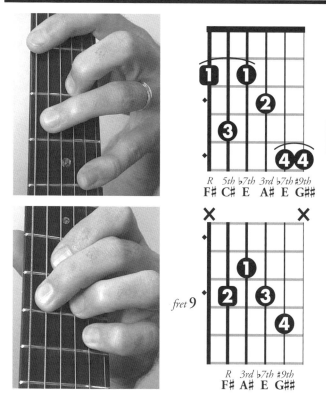

fret 9

R 3rd ♭7th #9th
F# A# E G##

F#9(♭5)

SCALE DEGREES: *R 3rd ♭5th ♭7th 9th*
CHORD TONES: F# A# C E G#

R 3rd ♭7th 9th ♭5th
F# A# E G# C

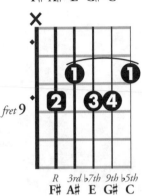

fret 9

R 3rd ♭7th 9th ♭5th
F# A# E G# C

F#9(#5)

SCALE DEGREES: *R 3rd #5th ♭7th 9th*
CHORD TONES: F# A# C## E G#

R 3rd ♭7th 9th #5th
F# A# E G# C##

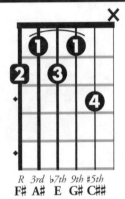

♭7th 3rd #5th 9th
E A# C## G#

F#
G♭

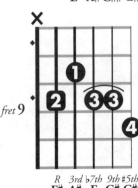

fret 9

R 3rd ♭7th 9th #5th
F# A# E G# C##

F♯dim7

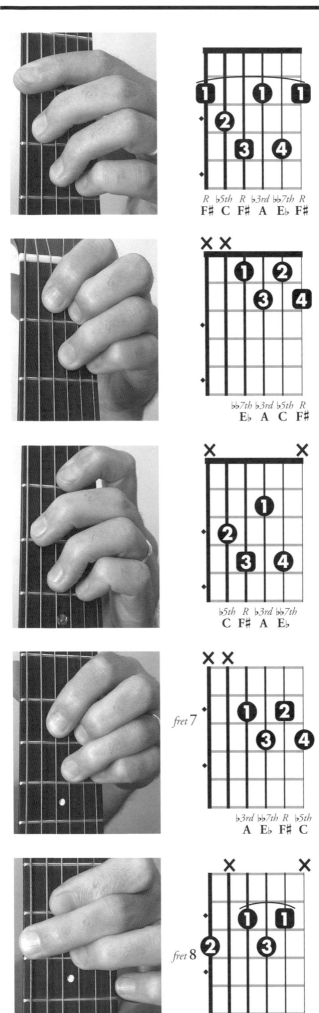

R ♭5th R ♭3rd ♭♭7th R
F♯ C F♯ A E♭ F♯

♭♭7th ♭3rd ♭5th R
E♭ A C F♯

♭5th R ♭3rd ♭♭7th
C F♯ A E♭

fret 7

♭3rd ♭♭7th R ♭5th
A E♭ F♯ C

F♯
G♭

fret 8

♭5th ♭3rd ♭♭7th R
C A E♭ F♯

G

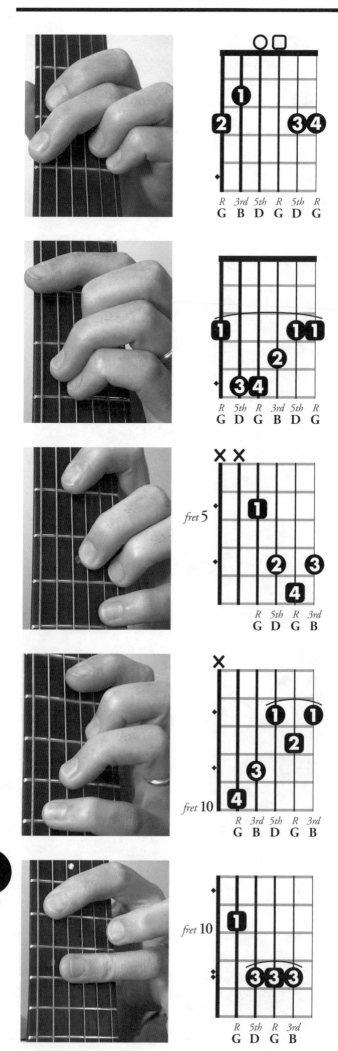

R 3rd 5th R 5th R
G B D G D G

R 5th R 3rd 5th R
G D G B D G

fret 5
R 5th R 3rd
G D G B

fret 10
R 3rd 5th R 3rd
G B D G B

fret 10
R 5th R 3rd
G D G B

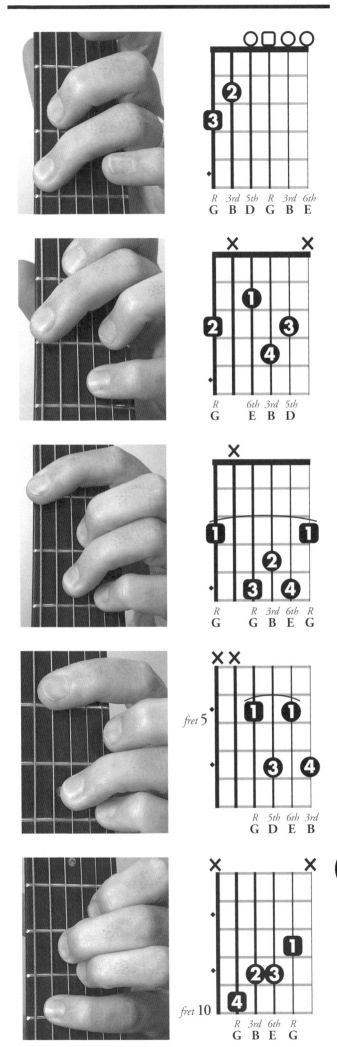

R 3rd 5th R 3rd 6th
G B D G B E

R 6th 3rd 5th
G E B D

R R 3rd 6th R
G G B E G

fret 5

R 5th 6th 3rd
G D E B

fret 10

R 3rd 6th R
G B E G

G

Gmaj7

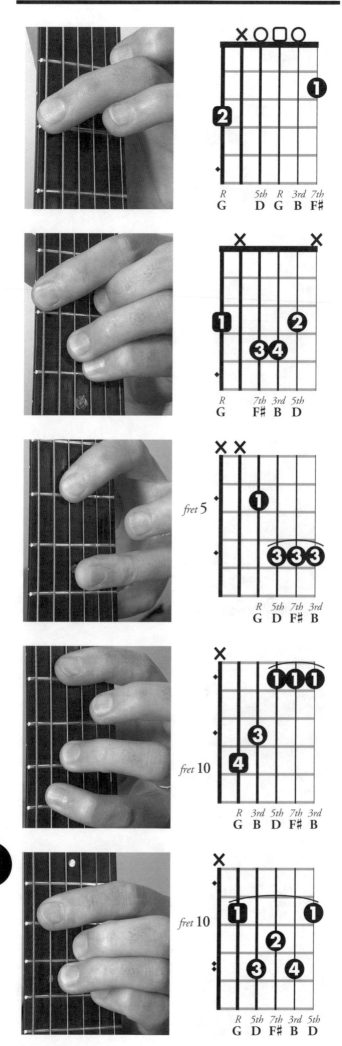

R   5th R   3rd 7th
G   D   G   B   F#

R   7th 3rd 5th
G   F#   B   D

fret 5

R   5th 7th 3rd
G   D   F#   B

fret 10

R   3rd 5th 7th 3rd
G   B   D   F#   B

G

fret 10

R   5th 7th 3rd 5th
G   D   F#   B   D

G(9)

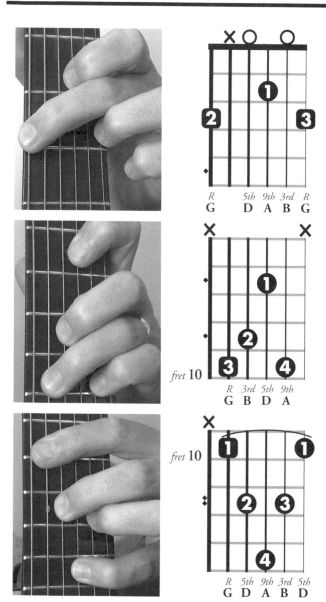

R		5th	9th	3rd	R
G		D	A	B	G

R	3rd	5th	9th
G	B	D	A

fret 10

R	5th	9th	3rd	5th
G	D	A	B	D

fret 10

Gmaj9

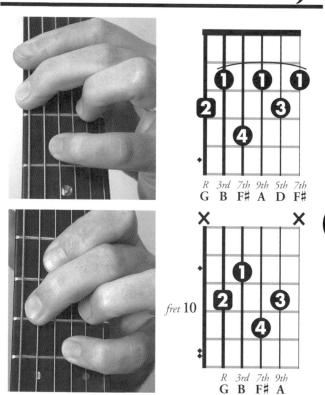

R	3rd	7th	9th	5th	7th
G	B	F♯	A	D	F♯

fret 10

R	3rd	7th	9th
G	B	F♯	A

G

Gmaj7(♯11)

SCALE DEGREES: *R 3rd 5th 7th ♯11th*
CHORD TONES: G B D F♯ C♯

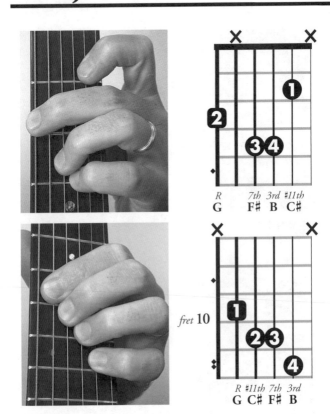

R		7th	3rd	♯11th
G		F♯	B	C♯

fret 10

R	♯11th	7th	3rd
G	C♯	F♯	B

G6/9

SCALE DEGREES: *R 3rd 5th 6th 9th*
CHORD TONES: G B D E A

R	3rd	6th	9th	5th	6th
G	B	E	A	D	E

R	3rd	6th	9th
G	B	E	A

fret 10

R	3rd	6th	9th	6th
G	B	E	A	E

G

SCALE DEGREES: *R 2nd 5th*
CHORD TONES: G A D

Gsus2

```
  ×  O
┌──┬──┬──┬──┐
├──┼──┼──┼──┤
│  │  │  ①  │
②  │  │  ③ ④
├──┼──┼──┼──┤
◆──┴──┴──┴──┘
```
R   5th 2nd 5th R
G   D A D G

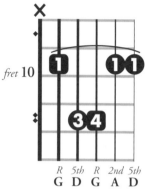

fret 10

```
  ×
┌──┬──┬──┬──┐
◆  │  │  │  │
│  ①  │  ① ①
├──┼──┼──┼──┤
◆  │  ③ ④  │
```
R 5th R 2nd 5th
G D G A D

SCALE DEGREES: *R 4th 5th*
CHORD TONES: G C D

Gsus4

```
        O □    ×
┌──┬──┬──┬──┐
│  │  │  ①  │
③ ④  │  │  │
├──┼──┼──┼──┤
◆──┴──┴──┴──┘
```
R 4th 5th R 4th
G C D G C

fret 5

```
┌──┬──┬──┬──┐
◆  ① ①  │  │
├──┼──┼──┼──┤
│  │  │  ③  │
◆  │  │  │ ④ ④
```
5th R 5th R 4th
D G D G C

fret 10

```
  ×
┌──┬──┬──┬──┐
│  ① ①  │  ①
├──┼──┼──┼──┤
◆  │  │  ③  │
│  │  │  │ ④
```
R 4th R 4th 5th
G C G C D

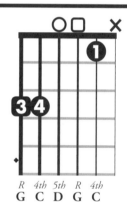
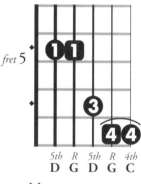
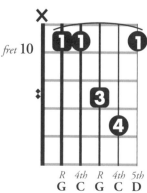

G

Gm

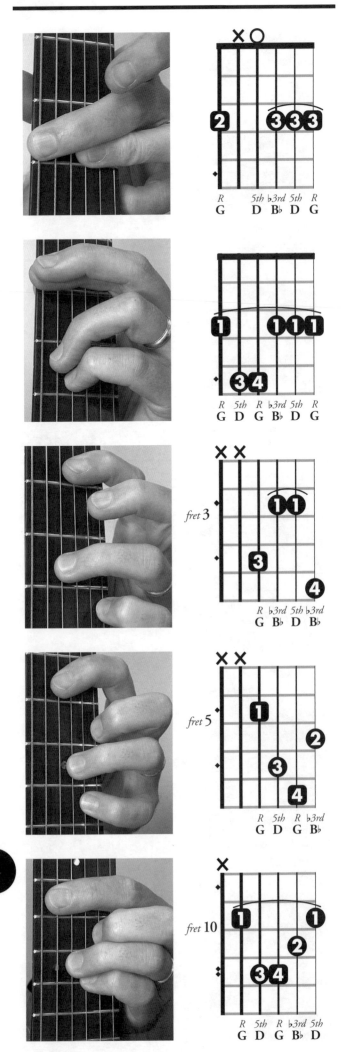

Gm6

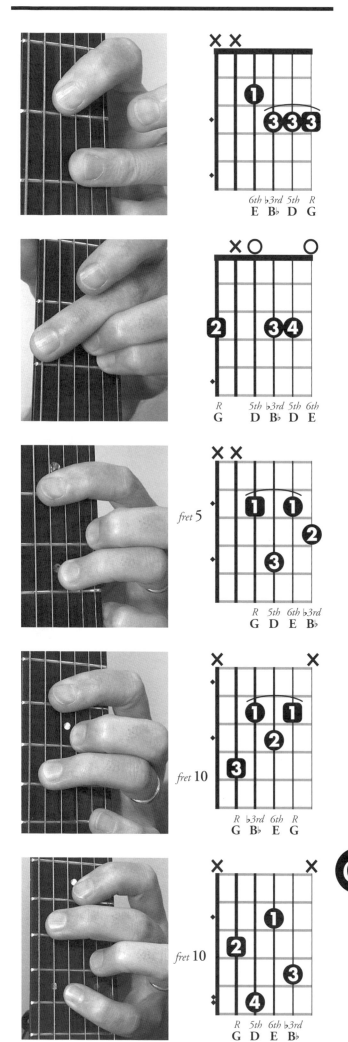

6th ♭3rd 5th R
E B♭ D G

R   5th ♭3rd 5th 6th
G   D B♭ D E

fret 5

R 5th 6th ♭3rd
G D E B♭

fret 10

R ♭3rd 6th R
G B♭ E G

G

fret 10

R 5th 6th ♭3rd
G D E B♭

Gm7

SCALE DEGREES: R ♭3rd 5th ♭7th
CHORD TONES: G B♭ D F

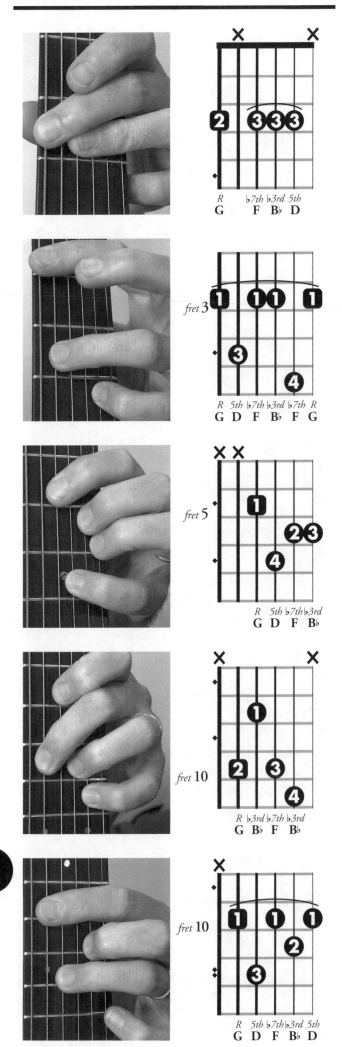

R ♭7th ♭3rd 5th
G F B♭ D

fret 3

R 5th ♭7th ♭3rd ♭7th R
G D F B♭ F G

fret 5

R 5th ♭7th ♭3rd
G D F B♭

fret 10

R ♭3rd ♭7th ♭3rd
G B♭ F B♭

fret 10

R 5th ♭7th ♭3rd 5th
G D F B♭ D

SCALE DEGREES: *R ♭3rd ♭5th ♭7th*
CHORD TONES: G B♭ D♭ F

Gm7(♭5)

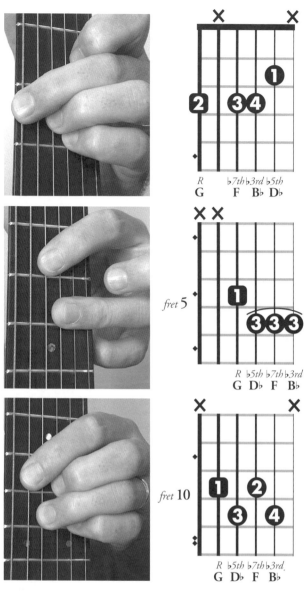

R ♭7th ♭3rd ♭5th
G   F   B♭   D♭

fret 5

R ♭5th ♭7th ♭3rd
G D♭   F   B♭

fret 10

R ♭5th ♭7th ♭3rd
G D♭   F   B♭

SCALE DEGREES: *R ♭3rd 5th ♭7th 9th*
CHORD TONES: G B♭ D F A

Gm9

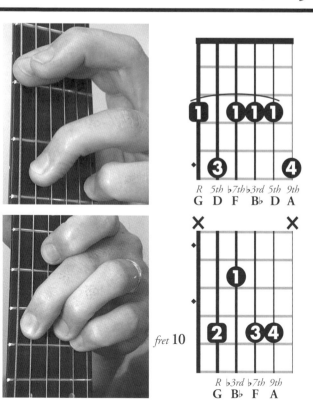

R 5th ♭7th ♭3rd 5th 9th
G   D   F   B♭   D   A

fret 10

R ♭3rd ♭7th 9th
G B♭   F   A

G

Gm(maj7)

SCALE DEGREES: R ♭3rd 5th 7th
CHORD TONES: G B♭ D F♯

R		5th	♭3rd	5th	7th
G		D	B♭	D	F♯

fret 10

R	5th	7th	♭3rd	5th
G	D	F♯	B♭	D

Gm(9)

SCALE DEGREES: R ♭3rd 5th 9th
CHORD TONES: G B♭ D A

R	5th	R	♭3rd	5th	9th
G	D	G	B♭	D	A

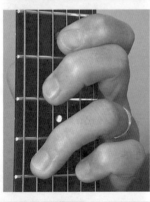

fret 10

R	♭3rd	5th	9th
G	B♭	D	A

fret 10

R	5th	9th	♭3rd	5th
G	D	A	B♭	D

G

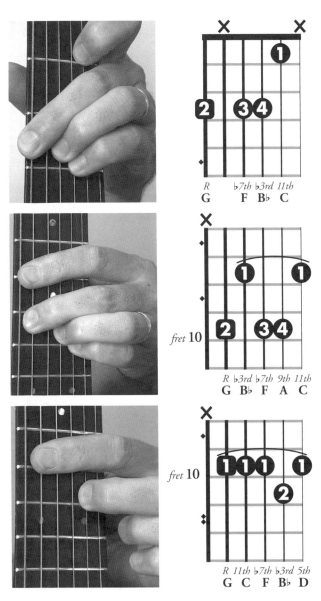

× ×

R		♭7th	♭3rd	11th
G		F	B♭	C

fret 10

R	♭3rd	♭7th	9th	11th
G	B♭	F	A	C

fret 10

R	11th	♭7th	♭3rd	5th
G	C	F	B♭	D

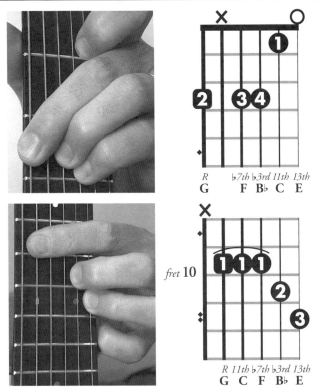

R		♭7th	♭3rd	11th	13th
G		F	B♭	C	E

fret 10

R	11th	♭7th	♭3rd	13th
G	C	F	B♭	E

G

G7

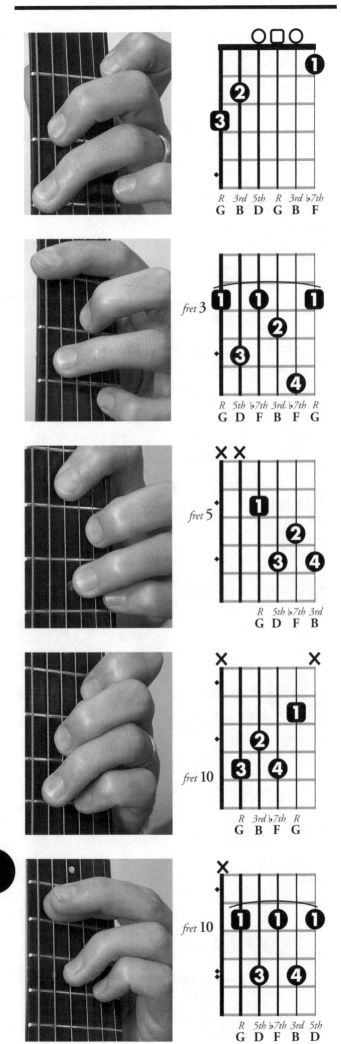

○ □ ○

R	3rd	5th	R	3rd	♭7th
G	B	D	G	B	F

fret 3

R	5th	♭7th	3rd.	♭7th	R
G	D	F	B	F	G

fret 5

R	5th	♭7th	3rd
G	D	F	B

fret 10

R	3rd	♭7th	R
G	B	F	G

fret 10

R	5th	♭7th	3rd	5th
G	D	F	B	D

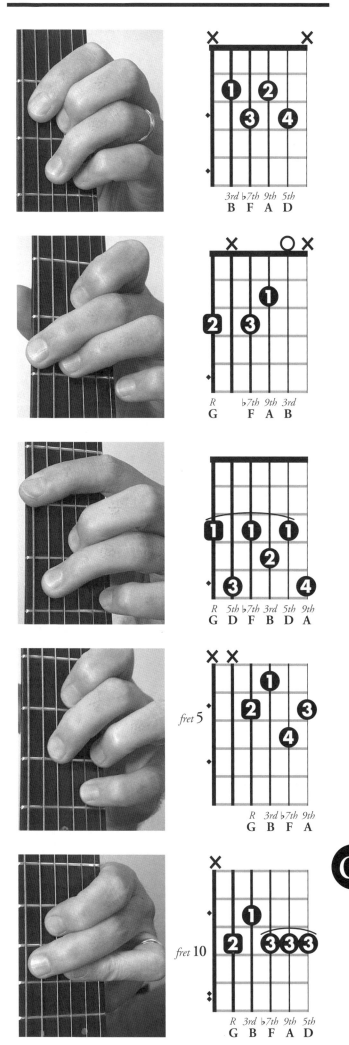

×   ×

3rd ♭7th 9th 5th
B   F   A   D

×   ○ ×

R   ♭7th 9th 3rd
G   F   A   B

R 5th ♭7th 3rd 5th 9th
G D F B D A

× ×

fret 5

R 3rd ♭7th 9th
G   B   F   A

×

fret 10

R 3rd ♭7th 9th 5th
G   B   F   A   D

G

G7sus4

SCALE DEGREES: R 4th 5th ♭7th
CHORD TONES: G C D F

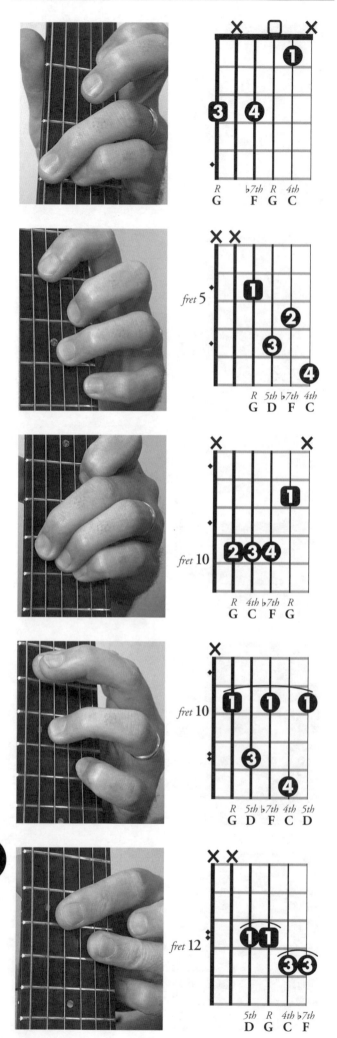

R   ♭7th R 4th
G   F G C

fret 5

R 5th ♭7th 4th
G D F C

fret 10

R 4th ♭7th R
G C F G

fret 10

R 5th ♭7th 4th 5th
G D F C D

fret 12

5th R 4th ♭7th
D G C F

SCALE DEGREES: *R 4th 5th ♭7th 9th*
CHORD TONES: G C D F A

G9sus4

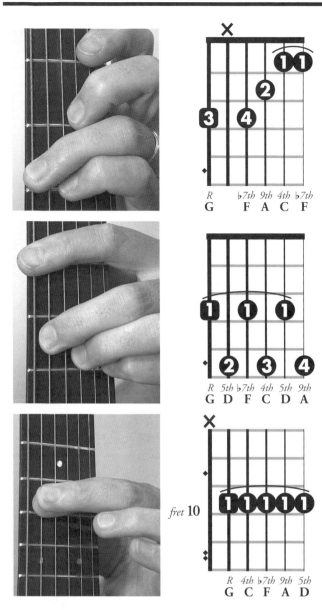

R   ♭7th 9th 4th ♭7th
G   F   A   C   F

R   5th ♭7th 4th 5th 9th
G   D   F   C   D   A

fret 10

R   4th ♭7th 9th 5th
G   C   F   A   D

SCALE DEGREES: *R 3rd 5th ♭7th 9th 11th 13th*
CHORD TONES: G B D F A C E

G13

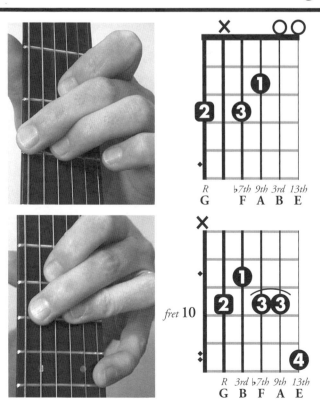

R   ♭7th 9th 3rd 13th
G   F   A   B   E

fret 10

R   3rd ♭7th 9th 13th
G   B   F   A   E

G

G7(♭5)

SCALE DEGREES: R 3rd ♭5th ♭7th
CHORD TONES: G B D♭ F

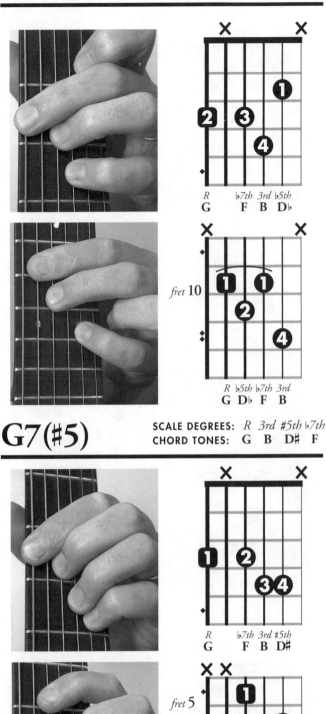

	R	♭7th	3rd	♭5th
	G	F	B	D♭

fret 10

R	♭5th	♭7th	3rd
G	D♭	F	B

G7(♯5)

SCALE DEGREES: R 3rd ♯5th ♭7th
CHORD TONES: G B D♯ F

R		♭7th	3rd	♯5th
G		F	B	D♯

fret 5

R	♯5th	♭7th	3rd
G	D♯	F	B

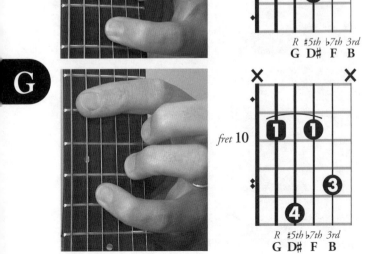

fret 10

R	♯5th	♭7th	3rd
G	D♯	F	B

G

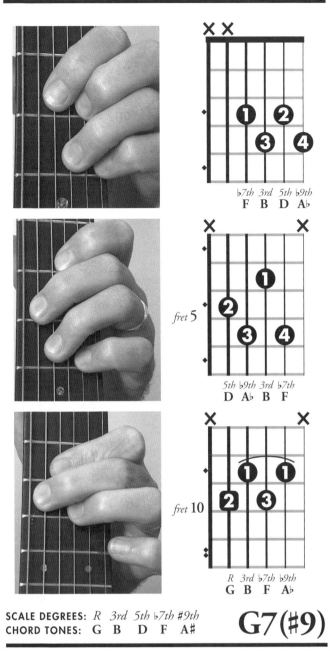

♭7th 3rd 5th ♭9th
F   B   D   A♭

fret 5

5th ♭9th 3rd ♭7th
D   A♭   B   F

fret 10

R   3rd ♭7th ♭9th
G   B   F   A♭

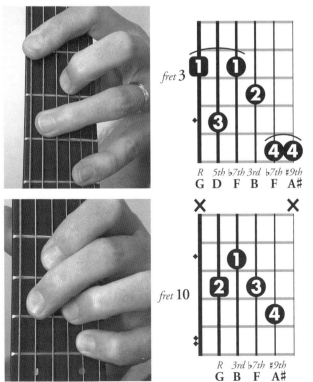

fret 3

R 5th ♭7th 3rd ♭7th #9th
G D   F   B   F   A#

fret 10

R   3rd ♭7th #9th
G   B   F   A#

G

G9(♭5)

SCALE DEGREES: *R 3rd ♭5th ♭7th 9th*
CHORD TONES: G B D♭ F A

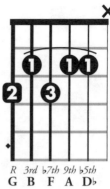

R 3rd ♭7th 9th ♭5th
G B F A D♭

fret 10

R 3rd ♭7th 9th ♭5th
G B F A D♭

G9(♯5)

SCALE DEGREES: *R 3rd ♯5th ♭7th 9th*
CHORD TONES: G B D♯ F A

R 3rd ♭7th 9th ♯5th
G B F A D♯

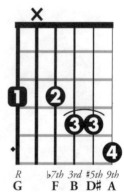

R ♭7th 3rd ♯5th 9th
G F B D♯ A

G

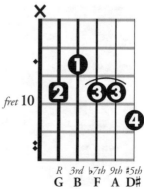

fret 10

R 3rd ♭7th 9th ♯5th
G B F A D♯

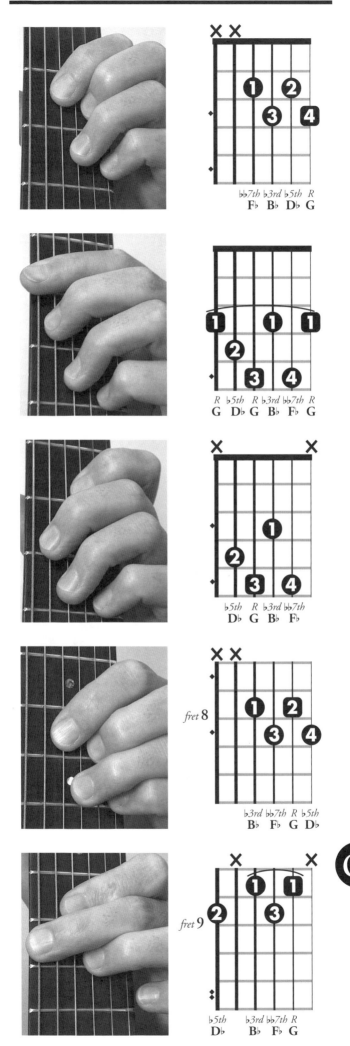

× ×

❶ ❷
❸ ❹

♭♭7th ♭3rd ♭5th R
F♭ B♭ D♭ G

❶ ❶ ❶
❷
❸ ❹

R ♭5th R ♭3rd ♭♭7th R
G D♭ G B♭ F♭ G

× ×

❶
❷
❸ ❹

♭5th R ♭3rd ♭♭7th
D♭ G B♭ F♭

× ×

fret 8

❶ ❷
❸ ❹

♭3rd ♭♭7th R ♭5th
B♭ F♭ G D♭

× ×

fret 9

❷ ❶ ❶
❸

♭5th ♭3rd ♭♭7th R
D♭ B♭ F♭ G

G

A♭

R 3rd 5th R 3rd
A♭ C E♭ A♭ C

fret 4

R 5th R 3rd 5th R
A♭ E♭ A♭ C E♭ A♭

fret 6

R 5th R 3rd
A♭ E♭ A♭ C

fret 11

R 3rd 5th R 3rd
A♭ C E♭ A♭ C

fret 11

R 5th R 3rd
A♭ E♭ A♭ C

G#
A♭

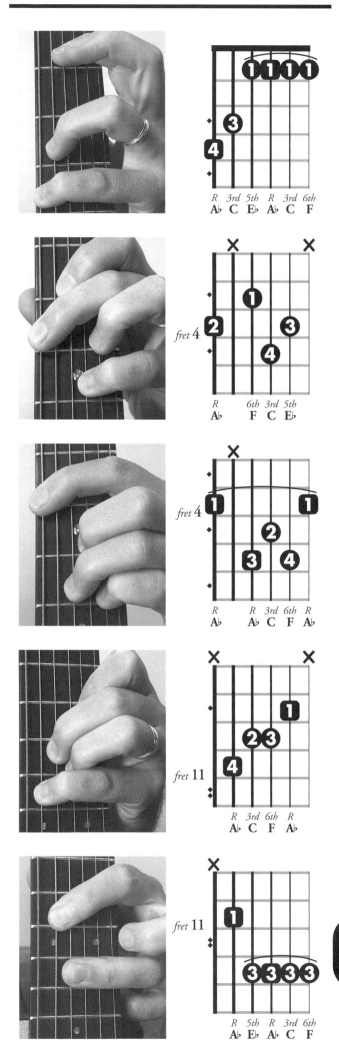

A♭maj7

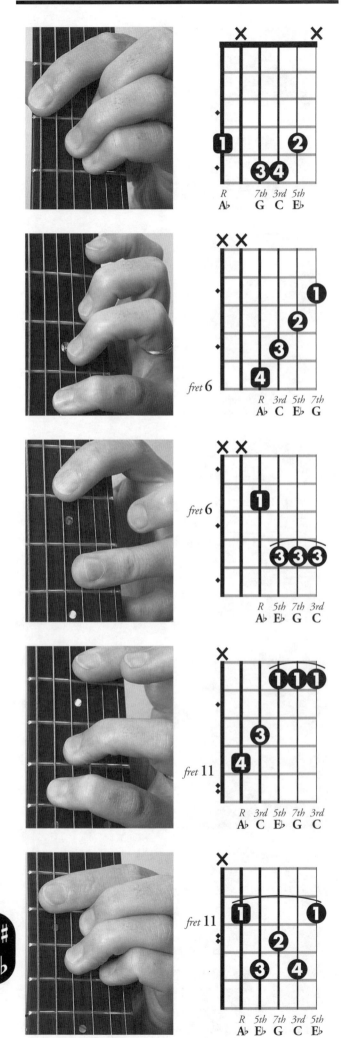

R   7th 3rd 5th
A♭   G   C E♭

fret 6
R   3rd 5th 7th
A♭ C E♭ G

fret 6
R   5th 7th 3rd
A♭ E♭ G   C

fret 11
R   3rd 5th 7th 3rd
A♭ C E♭ G   C

fret 11
R   5th 7th 3rd 5th
A♭ E♭ G   C E♭

G#
A♭

SCALE DEGREES: R 3rd 5th 9th
CHORD TONES: Ab C Eb Bb

Ab(9)

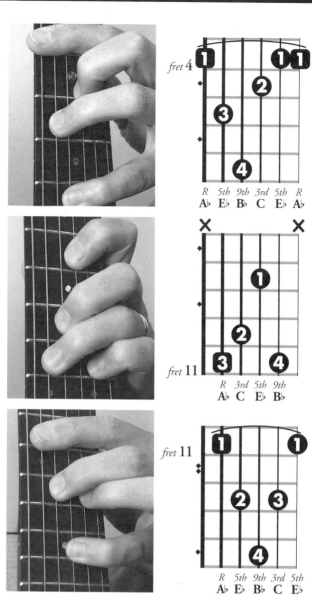

fret 4

R	5th	9th	3rd	5th	R
Ab	Eb	Bb	C	Eb	Ab

fret 11

R	3rd	5th	9th
Ab	C	Eb	Bb

fret 11

R	5th	9th	3rd	5th
Ab	Eb	Bb	C	Eb

SCALE DEGREES: R 3rd 5th 7th 9th
CHORD TONES: Ab C Eb G Bb

Abmaj9

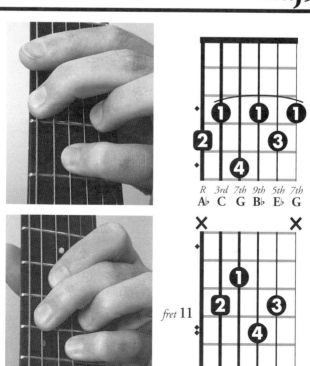

R	3rd	7th	9th	5th	7th
Ab	C	G	Bb	Eb	G

fret 11

R	3rd	7th	9th
Ab	C	G	Bb

G#
Ab

A♭maj7(#11)

SCALE DEGREES: R 3rd 5th 7th #11th
CHORD TONES: A♭ C E♭ G D

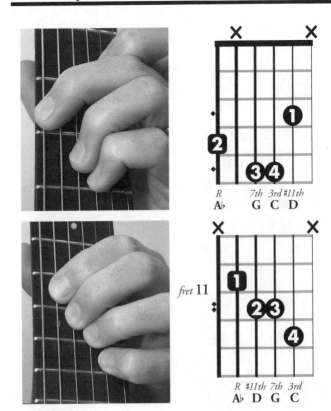

A♭6/9

SCALE DEGREES: R 3rd 5th 6th 9th
CHORD TONES: A♭ C E♭ F B♭

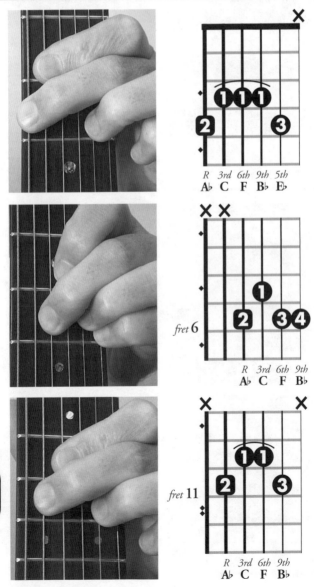

G#
A♭

SCALE DEGREES: *R 2nd 5th*
CHORD TONES: A♭ B♭ E♭

A♭**sus2**

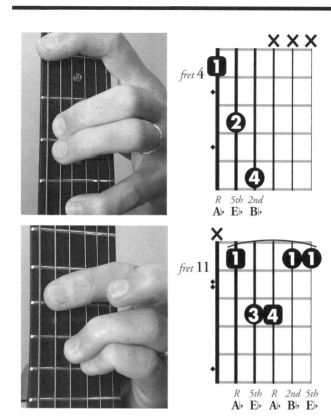

R   5th 2nd
A♭ E♭   B♭

R   5th R   2nd 5th
A♭ E♭   A♭ B♭   E♭

SCALE DEGREES: *R 4th 5th*
CHORD TONES: A♭ D♭ E♭

A♭**sus4**

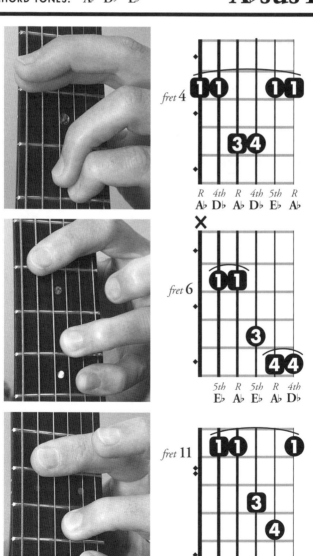

R   4th R   4th 5th R
A♭ D♭   A♭ D♭   E♭   A♭

5th R   5th R   4th
E♭   A♭ E♭   A♭ D♭

R   4th R   4th 5th
A♭ D♭   A♭ D♭   E♭

G#
A♭

A♭m

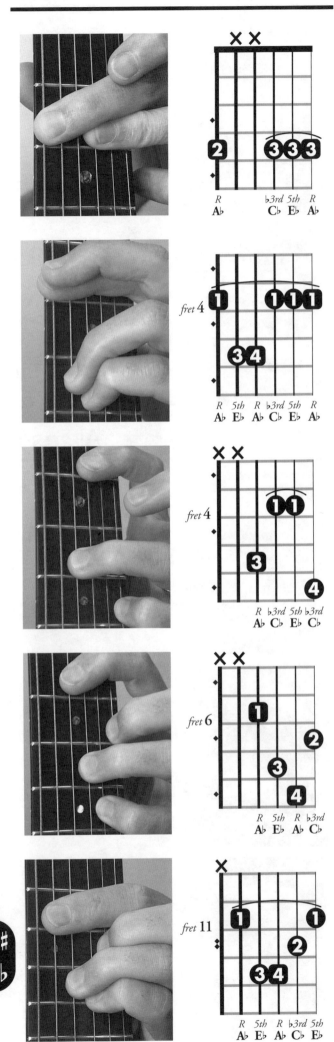

R   ♭3rd 5th R
A♭   C♭ E♭ A♭

fret 4

R 5th R ♭3rd 5th R
A♭ E♭ A♭ C♭ E♭ A♭

fret 4

R ♭3rd 5th ♭3rd
A♭ C♭ E♭ C♭

fret 6

R 5th R ♭3rd
A♭ E♭ A♭ C♭

fret 11

R 5th R ♭3rd 5th
A♭ E♭ A♭ C♭ E♭

G#
A♭

SCALE DEGREES: *R ♭3rd 5th 6th*
CHORD TONES: **A♭ C♭ E♭ F**

A♭m6

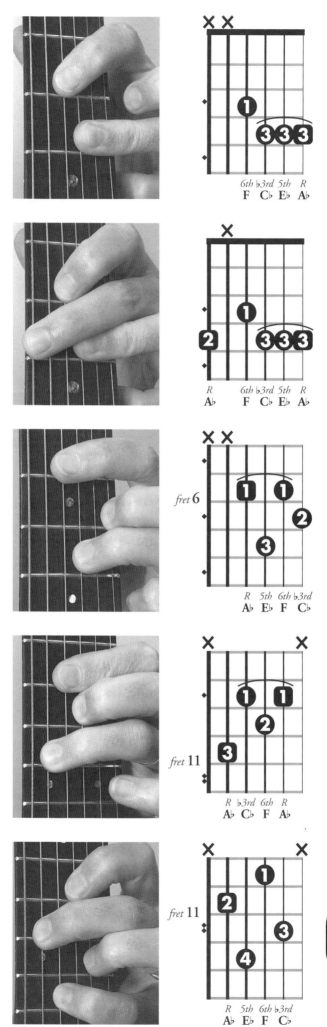

F C♭ E♭ A♭
6th ♭3rd 5th R

A♭ F C♭ E♭ A♭
R 6th ♭3rd 5th R

fret 6

A♭ E♭ F C♭
R 5th 6th ♭3rd

fret 11

A♭ C♭ F A♭
R ♭3rd 6th R

fret 11

A♭ E♭ F C♭
R 5th 6th ♭3rd

G#
A♭

A♭m7

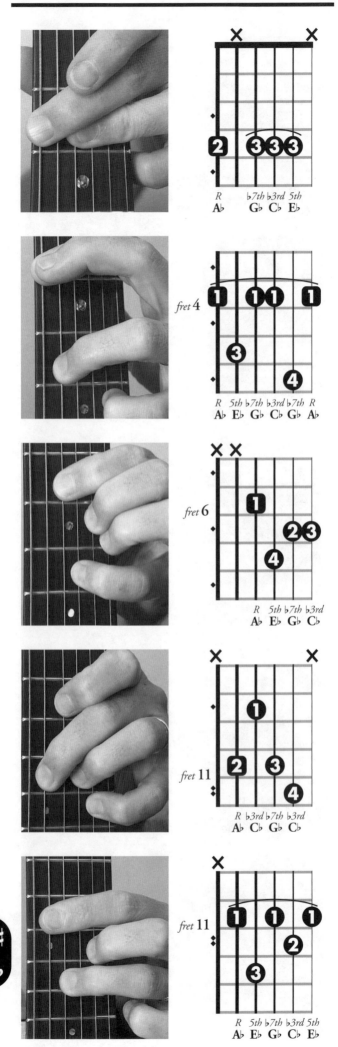

×   ×

2   3 3 3

R   ♭7th ♭3rd 5th
A♭   G♭ C♭ E♭

---

fret 4

1   1 1   1
3
4

R 5th ♭7th ♭3rd ♭7th R
A♭ E♭ G♭ C♭ G♭ A♭

× ×

fret 6

1
2 3
4

R 5th ♭7th ♭3rd
A♭ E♭ G♭ C♭

×   ×

fret 11

1
2   3
4

R ♭3rd ♭7th ♭3rd
A♭ C♭ G♭ C♭

×

fret 11

1   1   1
2
3

R 5th ♭7th ♭3rd 5th
A♭ E♭ G♭ C♭ E♭

G♯
A♭

SCALE DEGREES: R ♭3rd ♭5th ♭7th
CHORD TONES: A♭ C♭ E♭♭ G♭

A♭m7(♭5)

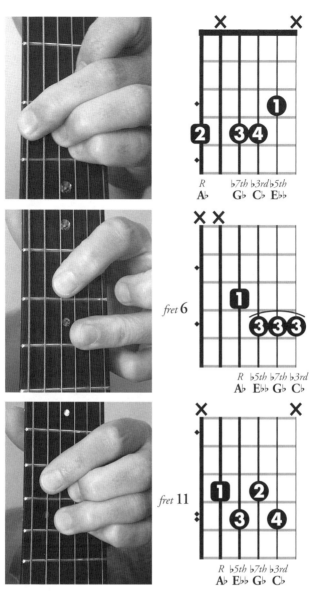

R ♭7th ♭3rd ♭5th
A♭ G♭ C♭ E♭♭

fret 6

R ♭5th ♭7th ♭3rd
A♭ E♭♭ G♭ C♭

fret 11

R ♭5th ♭7th ♭3rd
A♭ E♭♭ G♭ C♭

SCALE DEGREES: R ♭3rd 5th ♭7th 9th
CHORD TONES: A♭ C♭ E♭ G♭ B♭

A♭m9

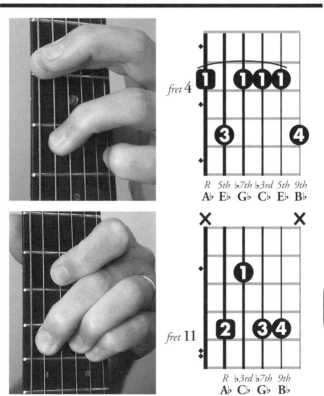

fret 4

R 5th ♭7th ♭3rd 5th 9th
A♭ E♭ G♭ C♭ E♭ B♭

fret 11

R ♭3rd ♭7th 9th
A♭ C♭ G♭ B♭

G#
A♭

A♭m(maj7)

SCALE DEGREES: R ♭3rd 5th 7th
CHORD TONES: A♭ C♭ E♭ G

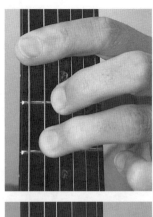

fret 4

R	5th	7th	♭3rd	5th
A♭	E♭	G	C♭	E♭

fret 11

R	5th	7th	♭3rd	5th
A♭	E♭	G	C♭	E♭

A♭m(9)

SCALE DEGREES: R ♭3rd 5th 9th
CHORD TONES: A♭ C♭ E♭ B♭

fret 4

R	5th	R	♭3rd	5th	9th
A♭	E♭	A♭	C♭	E♭	B♭

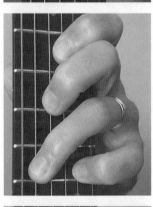

fret 11

R	♭3rd	5th	9th
A♭	C♭	E♭	B♭

fret 11

R	5th	9th	♭3rd	5th
A♭	E♭	B♭	C♭	E♭

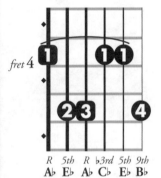
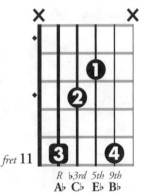
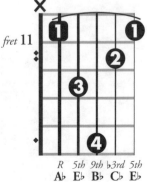

SCALE DEGREES: *R ♭3rd 5th ♭7th 9th 11th*
CHORD TONES: A♭ C♭ E♭ G♭ B♭ D♭

A♭m11

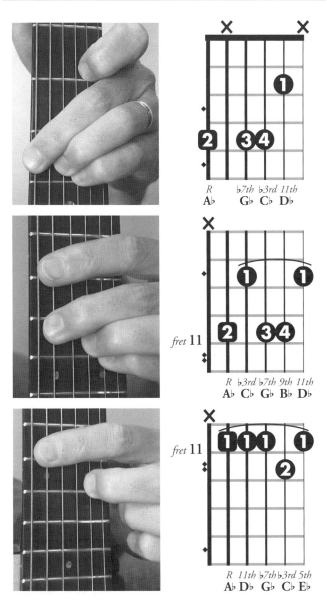

R		♭7th	♭3rd	11th
A♭		G♭	C♭	D♭

fret 11

R	♭3rd	♭7th	9th	11th
A♭	C♭	G♭	B♭	D♭

fret 11

R	11th	♭7th	♭3rd	5th
A♭	D♭	G♭	C♭	E♭

SCALE DEGREES: *R ♭3rd 5th ♭7th 9th 11th 13th*
CHORD TONES: A♭ C♭ E♭ G♭ B♭ D♭ F

A♭m13

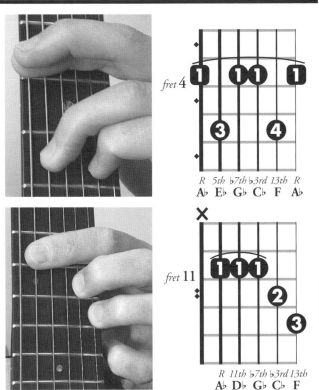

fret 4

R	5th	♭7th	♭3rd	13th	R
A♭	E♭	G♭	C♭	F	A♭

fret 11

R	11th	♭7th	♭3rd	13th
A♭	D♭	G♭	C♭	F

G♯
A♭

A♭7

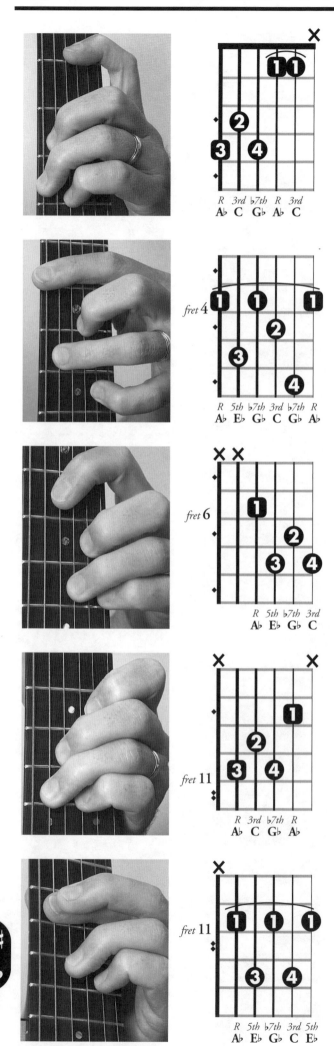

R 3rd ♭7th R 3rd
A♭ C G♭ A♭ C

fret 4

R 5th ♭7th 3rd ♭7th R
A♭ E♭ G♭ C G♭ A♭

fret 6

R 5th ♭7th 3rd
A♭ E♭ G♭ C

fret 11

R 3rd ♭7th R
A♭ C G♭ A♭

fret 11

R 5th ♭7th 3rd 5th
A♭ E♭ G♭ C E♭

G#
A♭

A♭9

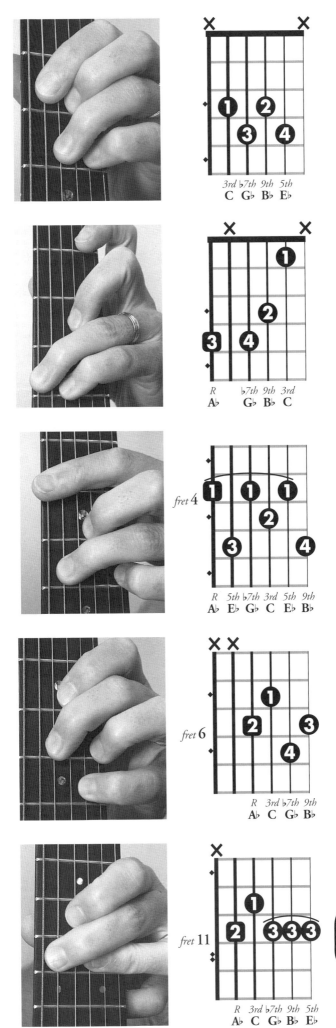

3rd ♭7th 9th 5th
C G♭ B♭ E♭

R ♭7th 9th 3rd
A♭ G♭ B♭ C

fret 4

R 5th ♭7th 3rd 5th 9th
A♭ E♭ G♭ C E♭ B♭

fret 6

R 3rd ♭7th 9th
A♭ C G♭ B♭

fret 11

R 3rd ♭7th 9th 5th
A♭ C G♭ B♭ E♭

G♯
A♭

A♭7sus4

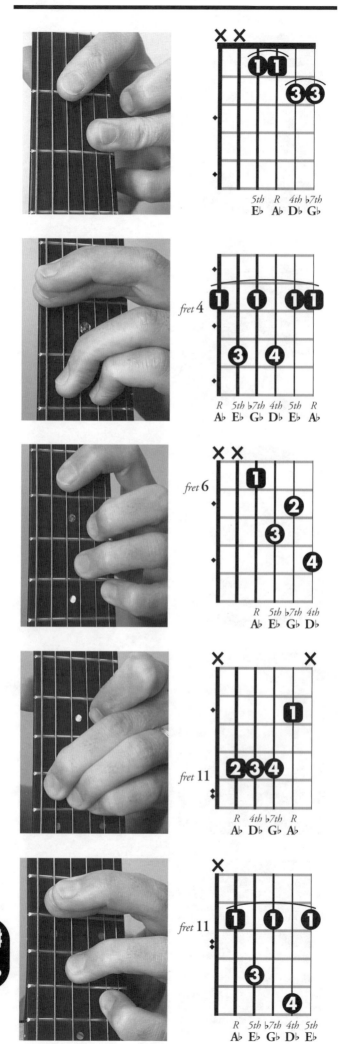

5th R   4th ♭7th
E♭ A♭ D♭ G♭

fret 4

R 5th ♭7th 4th 5th R
A♭ E♭ G♭ D♭ E♭ A♭

fret 6

R 5th ♭7th 4th
A♭ E♭ G♭ D♭

fret 11

R 4th ♭7th R
A♭ D♭ G♭ A♭

fret 11

R 5th ♭7th 4th 5th
A♭ E♭ G♭ D♭ E♭

G#
A♭

SCALE DEGREES: R 4th 5th ♭7th 9th
CHORD TONES: A♭ D♭ E♭ G♭ B♭

A♭9sus4

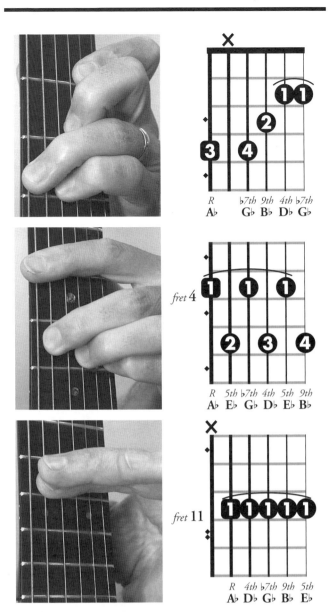

R 　　♭7th 9th 4th ♭7th
A♭ 　　G♭ B♭ D♭ G♭

fret 4

R 5th ♭7th 4th 5th 9th
A♭ E♭ G♭ D♭ E♭ B♭

fret 11

R 4th ♭7th 9th 5th
A♭ D♭ G♭ B♭ E♭

SCALE DEGREES: R 3rd 5th ♭7th 9th 11th 13th
CHORD TONES: A♭ C E♭ G♭ B♭ D♭ F

A♭13

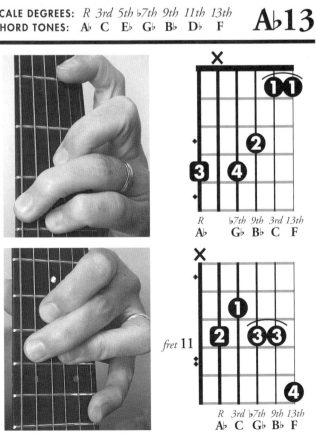

R 　　♭7th 9th 3rd 13th
A♭ 　　G♭ B♭ C F

fret 11

R 3rd ♭7th 9th 13th
A♭ C G♭ B♭ F

G♭
A♭

A♭7(♭5)

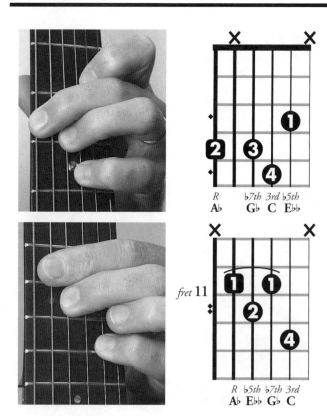

R   ♭7th 3rd ♭5th
A♭   G♭ C E♭♭

fret 11

R ♭5th ♭7th 3rd
A♭ E♭♭ G♭ C

A♭7(#5)

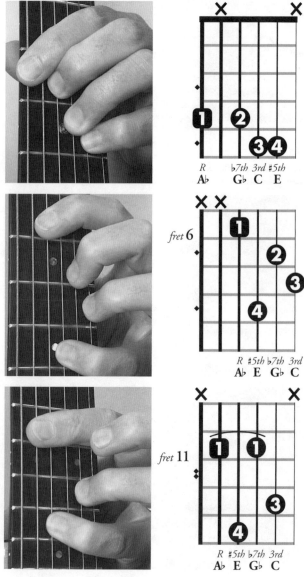

R   ♭7th 3rd #5th
A♭   G♭ C E

fret 6

R #5th ♭7th 3rd
A♭ E G♭ C

fret 11

R #5th ♭7th 3rd
A♭ E G♭ C

G#
A♭

A♭7(♭9)

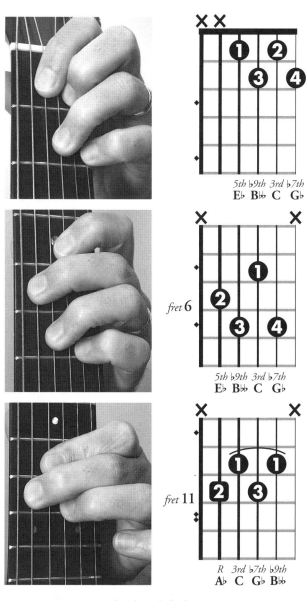

5th ♭9th 3rd ♭7th
E♭ B♭♭ C G♭

fret 6

5th ♭9th 3rd ♭7th
E♭ B♭♭ C G♭

fret 11

R 3rd ♭7th ♭9th
A♭ C G♭ B♭♭

A♭7(#9)

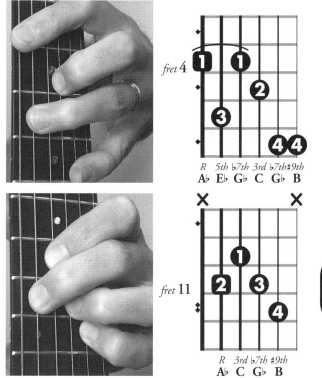

fret 4

R 5th ♭7th 3rd ♭7th #9th
A♭ E♭ G♭ C G♭ B

fret 11

R 3rd ♭7th #9th
A♭ C G♭ B

G#
A♭

A♭9(♭5)

SCALE DEGREES: *R 3rd ♭5th ♭7th 9th*
CHORD TONES: A♭ C E♭♭ G♭ B♭

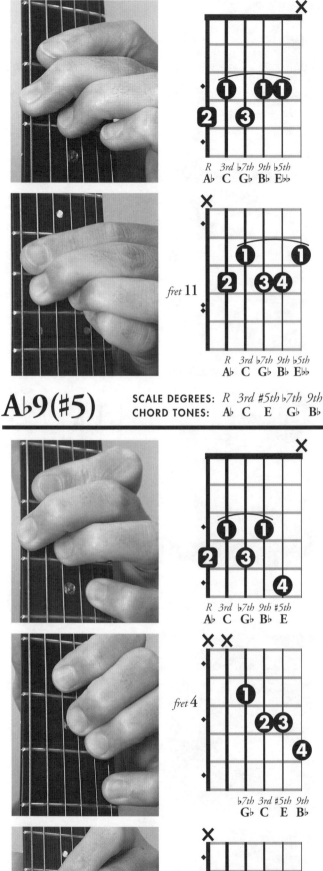

R 3rd ♭7th 9th ♭5th
A♭ C G♭ B♭ E♭♭

fret 11

R 3rd ♭7th 9th ♭5th
A♭ C G♭ B♭ E♭♭

A♭9(♯5)

SCALE DEGREES: *R 3rd ♯5th ♭7th 9th*
CHORD TONES: A♭ C E G♭ B♭

R 3rd ♭7th 9th ♯5th
A♭ C G♭ B♭ E

fret 4

♭7th 3rd ♯5th 9th
G♭ C E B♭

fret 11

R 3rd ♭7th 9th ♯5th
A♭ C G♭ B♭ E

G♯
A♭

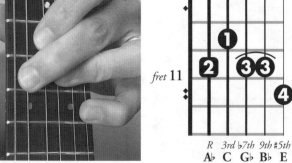

A♭dim7

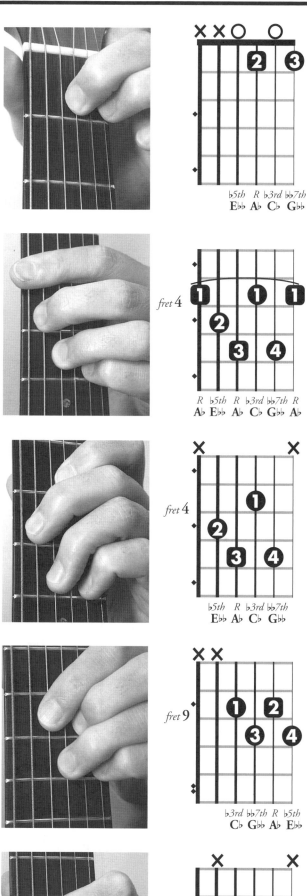

× × ○   ○

♭5th R ♭3rd ♭♭7th
E♭♭ A♭ C♭ G♭♭

fret 4

R ♭5th R ♭3rd ♭♭7th R
A♭ E♭♭ A♭ C♭ G♭♭ A♭

×   ×

fret 4

♭5th R ♭3rd ♭♭7th
E♭♭ A♭ C♭ G♭♭

× ×

fret 9

♭3rd ♭♭7th R ♭5th
C♭ G♭♭ A♭ E♭♭

× × ×

fret 10

♭5th   ♭3rd ♭♭7th R
E♭♭   C♭ G♭♭ A♭

G#
A♭

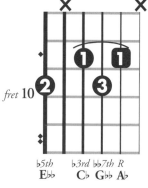

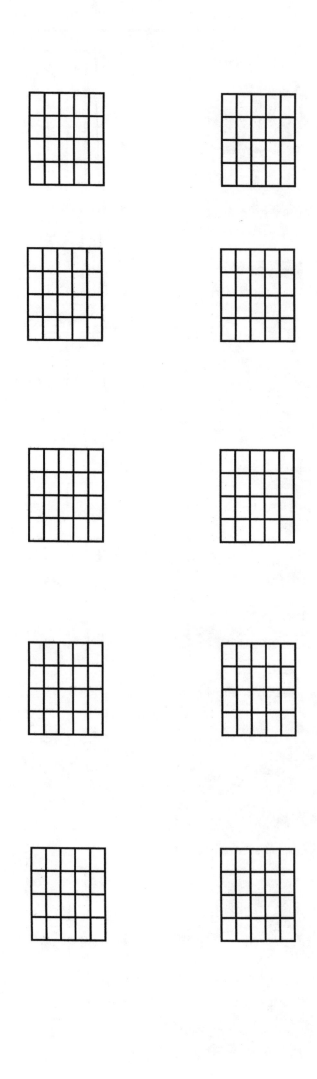

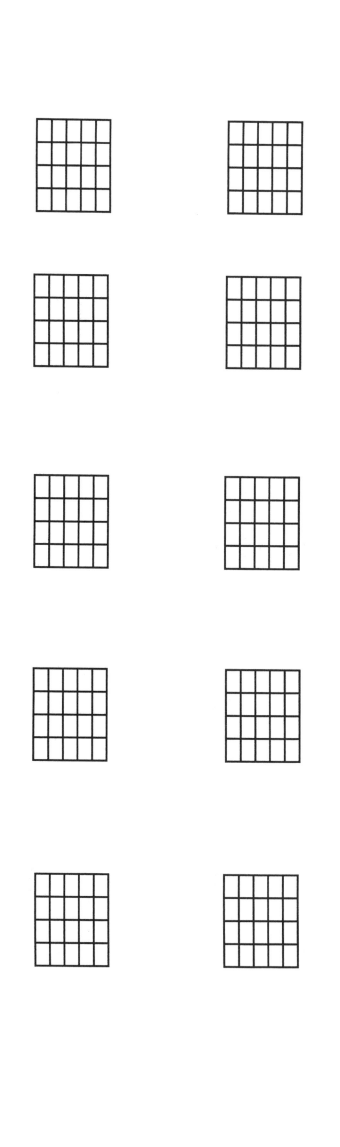

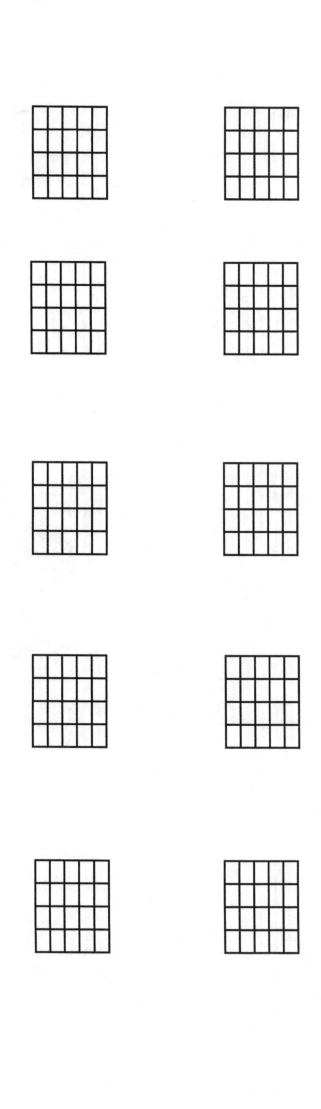